stitched in time

stitched in time

MEMORY-KEEPING PROJECTS TO SEW AND SHARE

FROM THE CREATOR OF
Posie Gets Cozy

Alicia Paulson

POTTER
CRAFT

NEW YORK

CONTRIBUTORS:

PHOTOGRAPHY BY Alicia Paulson

ILLUSTRATIONS BY Alicia Paulson

TECHNICAL EDITING BY Ellen Wheat

STYLING BY Alicia Paulson

MAKEUP BY April Ecklund

Photos for Friend Chandelier courtesy of Leslie Sophia Lindell

Knitted dog in photo for Sleepover Pillowcase by Kristina Therkildsen

Published in the United States by Potter Craft,
an imprint of the Crown Publishing Group,
a division of Random House, Inc., New York.
www.clarksonpotter.com
wwww.pottercraft.com

POTTER CRAFT and colophon is a registered trademark
of Random House, Inc.

Library of Congress Cataloging-in-Publication Data

Paulson, Alicia.
   Stitched in time : memory-keeping projects to sew and
share from the creator of Posie Gets Cozy / Alicia Paulson.
      p.   cm.
   Includes index.
   ISBN 978-0-307-40626-2
   1. Sewing.   2. Fancy work.   3. Souvenirs (Keepsakes)   I. Title.

   TT705.P348 2008
   746.4—dc22   2008003918

ISBN 978-0-307-40626-2

Printed in China

Design by Marysarah Quinn

10   9   8   7   6   5   4   3   2   1

First Edition

TO AUDREY

A good dog, queen of my heart

2001–2007

CONTENTS

INTRODUCTION

I have a terrible memory. That's frustrating, because I'm also a proud sentimentalist, and there are so many things, people, places, and events— even prosaic ones—I don't want to forget. I started making scrapbooks when I was a teenager, and I'm always delighted, amused, and nostalgic when I look back at volumes of old photos, souvenirs, or written things I've saved.

But these albums are stored on a shelf with a lot of other books at the far edge of my living room, and even though I have the best intentions and routinely remind myself to do it, I don't print out my digital photos regularly to add to the collection. The sheer volume of images encouraged by the idiotproofness of my camera overwhelms me—I can hardly keep them organized in their virtual folders. And there's a sort of chronological and comprehensive expectation with traditional scrapbooking and album-making that intimidates me—I don't know where to start, and if I do start, will I ever really finish?

There are other ways of remembering.

This collection of thirty special things to sew incorporates memory into every stitch. Using basic sewing, quilting, embroidery, and other craft skills, these projects take their inspirations from photos, drawings, souvenirs, vintage fabrics, and personalized details. More evocative than they are literal, these keepsakes evoke the feeling of a place and time rather than provide a documentation of events. Organized into three sections—For the Little Ones, For Every Day, and For Special Occasions—they are inspired by what it felt like to be at the farm that night last July, how it was to see the ballet for the very first time, which high-flying well wishes people sent for the baby when she was born. Some projects, like the Townhouse Growth Chart, become special only as they are used. Other projects, like the Wedding Guestbook Wall Hanging, commemorate important events in the most personal of ways. Still others, like the Cupcake Potholder, provide a sort of double-whammy souvenir: the "bronzing" of a piece of kid art in thread and fabric, and an everyday accessory for future afternoons spent baking together, to boot. And as useful everyday objects and decorations, these projects will live right in the thick of daily life, not stored away in an album on a shelf.

Have you ever come across something in your dresser that your mother—or grandmother, or aunt, or godmother—made for you? That tiny doll's dress can prompt as many memories and emotions as photos on a page or written words. If you show it to your mom, I bet she'll remember making it for you and get a little misty herself. Not only do the projects in this book offer a way to remember and honor special times, people, places, and events, but the act of working on them also becomes its own meaningful experience. Sewing things for others and for ourselves is a way of celebrating and honoring our families, our homes, and our days, both the special and the ordinary. There is good reason to take the time and make the effort to preserve and create memories with needle and thread. Sewing, like so many domestic arts, is so much more than a means to an end. It is an act of caring, and of taking care.

When you live with things—table linens, laundry bags, baby quilts—they become infused with the spirit of the home. When they are handmade, of special fabrics, with one-of-a-kind personalized details, they become even stronger stuff. I believe in art that is lived with, worn, slept under, used. I don't worry about whether it will last forever, though it might. I want it to work its magic here and now.

By Arden 8/1/07

THINGS TO KNOW BEFORE YOU SEW

For me, sewing is about enjoying the process, not necessarily making a perfectly executed heirloom. Perfection is relative. Though this book presumes a basic understanding of general sewing techniques, if you're new to sewing, don't get hung up on whether something seems easy or difficult—I believe in "love at first sight" when it comes to projects. Pick the one that really speaks to you and just jump in. Allow yourself the freedom to make mistakes—sometimes they can be the most endearing part of any finished project, and may provide further evidence of your unique personality and skills.

Dreaming about a project and shopping for supplies is a major part of the experience—sometimes it's even the best part (there, I said it). Make sure you have all the fabrics, notions, and tools you'll need to complete the project before you start. I think it's nice to clear a space, no matter how small, to dedicate to your work and to store your supplies. And while you're at it, briefly read through the directions for your chosen project to make sure you "get" what's going to happen. Having an idea of how the thing comes together will help you simply relax and enjoy the process.

Most of the projects in this book can be finished in a weekend or two by anyone with a basic knowledge of sewing. Many of them can be made either easier or more complicated based on your skill level and how much time you have. For each project, all materials and tools needed are listed, so you know what to gather before you start. Some of the projects incorporate techniques you may not be familiar with, so at the back of the book you'll find appendices that introduce you to general sewing techniques, hand-sewing, transferring photos to fabric, embroidery, appliqué, and freezer-paper stenciling. You will also find a section of templates for the projects that require them, a glossary of sewing terms, and a listing of online resources so you can find everything you need.

Please consider each of these projects a starting point. I hope you will further personalize them with your own ideas, skills, and memories, truly making them your own.

When I was a little girl, I had a wardrobe of wonders.
My mother was a magician with needle and thread. She
made my sisters and me butterfly-sleeved dresses with heart-
embroidered yokes, horseback-riding jackets with velvet collars.
We had wide-legged gauchos to go with the fashion boots
and ruffled nightgowns to go to the sleepovers. There were
organza pinafores to put over full-skirted lavender gingham
dresses, eyelet-trimmed calico bonnets to tie on for Easter,
and wool-plaid kilts to wear on Christmas. There was
absolutely nothing we could dream up that she couldn't,
or wouldn't, make for us.

Our room was peppered with handmade stuffed animals, pillowcases and matching bed jackets, crocheted blankets, embroideries she had finished and framed herself. Our favorite was a poster-sized piece of crewelwork of a blond girl in a blue dress standing under a canopy of pink cherry trees, their blossoms made of hundreds of pink wool French knots.

Our *parents'* room, on the other hand, was peppered with scraps of fabric, strands of thread, strips of trimmed seams, pins and pattern pieces. My mother kept her sewing machine and ironing board in her bedroom, and from the smallest of spaces, with the humblest of budgets, she made us what are still some of the loveliest gifts I can imagine. Even as a child, I appreciated my homemade things. Having dreamt up and requested some of them myself, having stood, knock-kneed, on more chairs while more skirts were hemmed than I could (almost) bear, having tagged along on the winding road from fabric store to finished piece more times than I could count, I knew about the time and effort that went into the stuff.

But as an adult, I see that what motivated my mother through a million stitches was love; I feel it every time I sew something special for a cherished child. I think there is no better way to honor the children in my life than to give them my best, most beautiful, most heartfelt handwork, my hopes and dreams for them gathered into the seams, my love tucked safely into every fold.

You need not be an accomplished seamstress to complete the heartfelt gifts in this section. Some, like the Kid's Drawing Softie, take more time and patience than skill, and others, like the Snail Onesie, can be made with simple embroidery stitches and just a few supplies. Oftentimes you'll find yourself racing against the clock with projects like these as you try to get them finished for a baby shower or a first sleepover. But I hope that you'll be able to adapt these projects to your (and your recipient's) own tastes, skills, and schedule in a way that allows you to really enjoy the process. I hope you'll love making them for the children you love as much as the kids will—if not today, then *some*day—love that they were made.

◀ *This embroidery was a crewelwork kit, done by my mom in the 1970s as a decoration for the bedroom I shared with my sisters.*

family tree

*I've always loved the tree imagery in old-fashioned genealogy charts.
This family tree design was inspired by early American folk art—simple, sweet, and traditional, but with a twist. This design contains different methods of appliqué—the birds and egg are done with turned edges slip-stitched to the foundation piece, and the tree, leaves, and nest are attached with fusible web and blanket stitches. But use any combination of appliqué methods you prefer. Mixing things up gives texture and dimension to this flat piece.*

Family Tree templates (page 146)

For foundation piece: One 18" x 18" (45.5cm x 45.5cm) piece of heavyweight canvas or denim-type fabric

For backing: One 18" x 20" (45.5cm x 51cm) piece of wool felt

For tree appliqué: One 9" x 9" (23cm x 23cm) piece of a brown cotton print

For other appliqués: An assortment of small-print cottons in Bird, Egg, and Leaf colors. (Bird and Egg fabric pieces should be big enough to fit into a 4" [10cm] embroidery hoop.) One 8 1/2" x 11" (21.5cm x 28cm) piece of heat-resistant template plastic

Dressmaker's chalk

Embroidery floss in assorted colors, to contrast with fabrics and buttons

Five 1/2" (13mm) colored buttons

Micron marker or fabric marker

Double-sided fusible web (like Heat 'n' Bond)

Spray starch

Small paintbrush

4" (10cm) embroidery hoop

Rotaty cutter

Self-healing cutting mat

Clear plastic ruler

Scalloped pinking shears

2 decorative twigs, either real wood or fake, about 24" (61cm) long and not more than 1/2" (13mm) wide at any point

FINISHED SIZE

17" x 18" (43cm x 45.5cm)

1. To prepare the turned-edge pieces, use the Family Tree templates and trace the Papa Bird, Mama Bird, and Egg shapes, right side up, onto the piece of heat-resistant plastic. Cut each shape out of the plastic and place it, right side up, onto the right side of the fabric. Trace around the shapes with dressmaker's chalk but don't cut them out yet. (Don't use a fabric marker here, since you will be pressing these pieces with a hot iron, which would make the ink permanent.) (See Appliqué [page 137].)

2. Using your computer, pick a simple font (I used Arial at 48-point size) to write out the parents' and baby's names in sizes that will fit on their respective shapes. Print out and transfer the names to the appliqué pieces, resizing and centering text as needed. Embroider each name onto its piece using a back stitch. (See Embroidery [page 134].) Cut out each piece, adding ¹/4" (6mm) seam allowance around shape.

3. Following the instructions in Appliqué (page 137), prepare all bird and egg pieces to be attached to the foundation piece by clipping, applying starch to, and pressing their edges under. Using the Tree, Leaf, and Nest templates, prepare the rest of the appliqué pieces by applying double-sided fusible

web (or adding a $^1/4$" [6mm] allowance and turning under their edges, if you prefer).

4. Lay out the appliqué pieces in a pleasing way on your foundation piece. Trace the placement of the elements with dressmaker's chalk so that it will be easy to remember what goes where. Set aside the appliqué pieces, except for the tree. Press the tree onto the foundation piece, following the manufacturer's instructions for your fusible web, then repeat for the leaves and nest. Pin the bird and egg pieces in place and attach them using a slip stitch. Using 2 strands of embroidery floss, decorate the edges of the leaves and tree trunk with blanket stitch. (See Hand-Sewing [page 130].)

5. For the nest and leaf veins, make long, strawlike straight stitches, using one strand of embroidery floss. Stitch the buttons to the foundation.

6. Trim the foundation piece to 16" x 16" (40.5cm x 40.5cm), keeping the design centered. Center and pin the foundation piece to the felt backing around all edges, centering it horizontally and vertically. There will be more felt extending beyond the top and bottom of the foundation piece than along the sides. Attach the foundation piece using blanket stitch and 3 strands of embroidery floss in a contrasting color. Trim the felt backing with pinking shears on the outside of the blanket stitches along the long edges. Turn the top and bottom edges under 1" (2.5cm) and machine-sew 3/4" (2cm) from folds to make casings for decorative twigs. Slide the twigs into the casings. To hang on the wall, balance the top twig on two small nails.

TIPS:

* Printed cotton calicos are my favorite type of fabrics for appliqué—tiny prints are best. For the embroidery, pick floss colors that will contrast with your fabrics. Tack a strand or two to your fabric piece and stand back to see whether the floss reads well. If not, experiment until you find combinations that let the embroidery really pop.

* If you want to include an older brother or sister, reduce one of the bigger birds on a copier.

* It might be nice to add each child's birthdate to the trunk of the tree, too.

Having put so much time and care into your handmade items, you should always consider labeling your work in some way. You can do what's easiest, and use a fine-tip permanent fabric marker to sign and date the back (or front) of your piece, but my favorite way of labeling things I've sewn is to sign and then embroider a small patch of separate fabric and appliqué it onto the back of my work (or the inside of a stocking, or inner flap of a book cover—whatever suits your fancy).

There is something really wonderful about making your own handwriting permanent in stitches. Practice a bit on paper so you can get a feel for the spacing. Add other design elements, like flowers or flourishes, or consider including more information: Add the recipient's name, the location in the which the item was made, your reason for making it, or even care instructions. When you like what you've written, transfer the design to the patch fabric and backstitch with one or two strands of embroidery floss (see Embroidery [page 134]).

If the item will be washed frequently or get a lot of wear and tear, consider fusing the patch to the finished project before appliquéing. To do this, simply cut out the finished label, adding a 1/4" (6mm) seam allowance. Then cut a patch of lightweight fusible interfacing in the exact shape of this piece. With the right side of the label and the fusible side of the interfacing together, pin around all edges, and machine-sew using a 1/4" (6mm) seam. Cut a small slit in the interfacing, just big enough to turn your label. Clip curves, trim corners, and turn the label right side out. Press the label to your finished item, then finish it off by slip stitching (see Hand-Sewing [page 130]) all around the patch by hand, with a sharp needle and regular thread.

There. *Now* you're done.

baby's arrival mobile

It's hard to know what to do with all the cards you receive for special occasions, such as a baby shower or the arrival of a new little one. The cards are so beautiful that it seems like a shame to tuck them into a box, rarely to be seen again. This simple project doesn't actually involve any sewing, but uses greeting cards, felt, scraps of fabric, and glue to make a charming, kite-inspired mobile that can be coordinated with the furnishings in baby's room. Hung above a crib or changing table (beyond the reach of little hands, of course), it's a reminder of all the good wishes and good friends in a tiny one's life.

MATERIALS

9 baby greeting cards

For felt linings: 9 pieces of felt in assorted colors, about $1/2$" (13mm) bigger on all sides than the trimmed cards

For tails: 36 scraps of assorted cotton prints, ripped or cut to about $1/2$" x 2" (13mm x 5cm)

For hanger: Four $1/4$" (6mm) wooden dowels, each 12" (30.5cm) long

For hanger bows: 2 yd (1.8m) of $1/2$"- (13mm-) wide silk ribbon

Rotary cutter

Self-healing cutting mat

Clear plastic ruler

Scalloped pinking shears

Heavyweight thread

Fabric glue

Acrylic paint

Clear varnish

1. To make the card shapes, cut the front of one card into a rectangle or a square, cropping the image in a pleasing way. Trace that shape onto the inside of the card, around the greeting and signature of its giver, and cut out both pieces. (To center the greeting and signature, hold the 2 pieces of the card against a sunny window when tracing.) Repeat this step for the other 8 cards.

2. Cut 9 lengths of thread 24" (61cm) long. Create the "tails" using square knots, tying 3 fabric strips to the lower portion of each length of the thread, first placing the upper tail about 9" (23cm) from the bottom end. Pull the thread firmly around the center of each fabric strip, bunching the fabric and making a "bow." Tie the second and third tails about 1" (2.5cm) below each previous tail. Set the 9 pieces aside.

3. Glue the front of the card to a piece of felt and trim the felt around the card with scalloped shears. Turn the piece over and lay a length of the fabric-tailed thread across the card diagonally, making a "kite" by keeping 1" (2.5cm) of space between the bottom corner of the kite and the top of the first tail. Let the long end of the thread trail from the opposite corner. Add a dab of glue near the 2 corners to secure the thread to the felt. Glue the greeting part of the card over the felt, sandwiching the thread between the layers. Repeat this step for the other 8 cards.

4. Paint the dowels with 2 coats of paint, and let them dry. Seal them with one coat of varnish and let them dry again. Stack the dowels in a square (see photo), and add a dab of glue at each corner to hold them in place while you tie their ends together in the next step. Let dry.

5. Cut 4 lengths of thread 18" (45.5cm) long. Tie one end of each length of thread to each corner of the stacked dowels. Pull the threads up from each corner evenly and tie them in a knot about 9" (23cm) from the ends. Double over the remaining 9" (23cm) and tie in a knot again at the first knot to make a loop to use for a hanger. Attach one card to the center of the mobile (below the hanger loop) with a knot. Add a dab of glue to secure all knots at the corners and at the hanging loop. Trim the ends of the thread close to the knots.

6. Attach each card-kite by the long end of its thread to the dowels, placing one at each corner and one in the middle of each dowel, spacing each one to balance evenly. It looks best if the card-kites at the four corners are a bit longer than the cards in the center of the dowels. When all the cards are balanced, tie each with a knot and add a dab of glue to secure. Trim the ends of the thread close to the knots. Tie the silk ribbon into bows at each corner and under the hanger loop.

TIPS:

* Practice trimming felt with shears on a few practice squares until you can make a clean corner. It's a little tricky, but once you've figured out where to start and stop your shears, it gets easier.

* Attach the mobile to a hook when tying on the cards, so you can see how everything balances and what needs to be rearranged. Take your time, and adjust things until the dowel hanger is parallel to the floor and the ceiling.

* Color copy the cards onto card stock if you don't want to cut up the originals.

snail onesie

*An outgrown onesie makes a great canvas, and when hung on a
sweet little vintage-y hanger, decorates baby's room in a charming way.
This adorable little onesie is just for display: The stabilizer applied to the
inside of the garment keeps the knit fabric from stretching when it's
embroidered and wouldn't be comfortable against tender newborn skin.*

Snail Onesie template (page 150)
Baby onesie

Iron-on tear-away stabilizer
Dressmaker's carbon paper
Fabric marker

4" (10cm) embroidery hoop
Embroidery floss in various
colors

1. Using your computer and a simple script font, print out baby's name and birthdate on paper (I used Send Flowers in 48- and 36-point sizes). Make sure that the widest part of your text is smaller than the width of the onesie, so you have a margin around the embroidery. Copy the Snail template at 100 percent. Cut out both the text and the snail, leaving about a 1/2" (13mm) margin around each, and tape pieces together, arranging to fit.

2. Iron the tear-away stabilizer to the wrong side of the front of the onesie, according to the manufacturer's directions.

3. Center the design, right side up, on the front of the onesie, and slide a piece of dressmaker's carbon, carbon side down, between the onesie and the design. Using a ballpoint pen, trace the design, transferring the outlines to the onesie. Retrace the lines with the fabric marker so you can see them more easily when embroidering.

4. Using 2 strands of embroidery floss, embroider the text with back stitches, the snail with chain stitches, and around the onesie's neck, arms, and legs with running stitches (see Hand-Sewing [page 130] and Embroidery [page 134]). When you're finished with all needlework, cut away most of the stabilizer and press the onesie with a warm iron.

TIPS:

* Choose a onesie with a soft, smooth finish and a tight weave, preferably 100 percent cotton. It will be easier to transfer the design to this knit fabric.

* To make the hanger, paint a simple wooden child's hanger with 2 coats of acrylic paint. Copy a sweet image from an old children's book, cut it out, and glue it to the hanger with white glue. Cover the entire hanger with 2 coats of varnish.

* You may choose to embroider your baby's birth weight and length on the onesie in addition to her birthdate.

silhouette stack

*This little profile is actually my own, snipped spontaneously by hand
by an artist at a street fair my parents attended when I was a toddler.
I like the juxtaposition of the rustic, ripped edges and the haphazard
arrangement of the fabric rectangles behind the formality of a classic silhouette.
This easy-to-make portrait can be hung directly on the wall or framed.
Choose colors and prints that coordinate but aren't too matchy—a little
tension in the piece is good, to keep it from looking too traditional.*

MATERIALS

For child's silhouette: Four 8 1/2" x
11" (21.5cm x 28cm) pieces of white
paper, taped together to form a 17" x
22" (43cm x 56cm) rectangle
For frame fabrics: Cotton prints,
ripped to the following dimensions:
One 12" x 14" (30.5cm x 35.5cm) piece
(fabric A)
One 11" x 13" (28cm x 33cm) piece
(fabric B)
One 10" x 12" (25.5cm x 30.5cm) piece
(fabric C)

One 9" x 11" (23cm x 28cm) piece
(fabric D)
One 8" x 10" (20.5cm x 25.5cm) piece
(fabric E)
One 6 1/2" x 8" (16.5cm x 20.5cm)
piece (fabric F)
For lining: One 12" x 14" (30.5cm x
35.5cm) piece of heavyweight fusible
web
For backing: One 13" x 15" (33cm x
38cm) piece of wool felt
Freezer paper

Small scissors or X-acto knife
Self-healing cutting mat
Fabric paint in a dark color
Small paintbrush
Embroidery floss to match color of
backing felt
Zigzag pinking shears

FINISHED SIZE
Approximately 12" x 14" (30.5cm x
35.5cm)

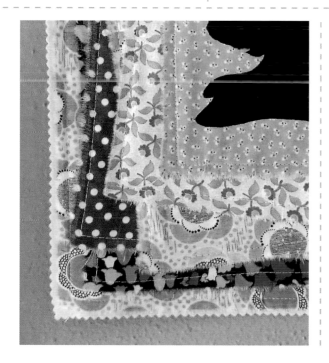

1. To make a silhouette, have your child sit in front
of the white piece of paper in a darkened room.
Place a bright lamp close to the child and trace the
outline of her shadow onto the paper. Use a copier
or a scanner to reduce the image to fit comfortably
on fabric F. Choose a print for that layer that has
tiny or subtle elements so it doesn't compete with
the silhouette.

2. To create the frame, rip the 6 fabric rectangles
A through F. To rip the fabric, make a tiny snip
at one corner to start. Gripping the fabric at each
side of the snip, rip hard and fast, going with the
grain. Measure from the top of the ripped edge to
the bottom, then snip, rip, and repeat for all 4 sides
of the rectangle. Remove any hanging threads, and

press. Repeat this process for the other 5 fabric layers of the frame. Trim the fusible web to be just slightly smaller than fabric piece A. Following the manufacturer's instructions, fuse the web to the back of fabric A.

3. Following the directions in Freezer-Paper Stenciling (page 139), paint the child's silhouette onto the front of fabric F. Let dry, then heat-set by ironing.

4. Place the fabric pieces in order in a stack, with piece A on the bottom and the silhouette (piece F) on the top, arranging the layers slightly off-center for a jaunty look. Then carefully lift the top layers (pieces C, D, E, and F) off the stack and set them aside. Pin piece B to piece A. Stitch around the edge of piece B about $1/4$" (6mm) in from the raw edge, pivoting at the corners. (For each layer, begin stitching at a place that will be overlapped by the next piece, and end with a few back stitches to secure.) Repeat for pieces C, D, and E. To attach the silhouette piece (F), place it centered and straight on top of the stack (see photo). Stitch around the edge of piece F as for the other pieces, starting and stopping in a bottom corner.

5. Press the entire stack and pin it, centered, to the felt backing. Stitch the stack to the felt piece around the edge of piece A, and trim the felt layer with pinking shears.

6. To make the stitches by which the piece will hang, using 2 strands of embroidery floss, make a knotless start (see Hand-Sewing [page 130]) on the back of the piece in an upper corner, securing the thread to the felt backing only. Make a $1/2$" (13mm) stitch, running the needle back under the felt backing but not all the way through the front of the piece, coming up where you started. Repeat the $1/2$" (13mm) stitch and fasten off, burying the tails of the thread (see Hand-Sewing [page 130]) under the felt and snipping off the ends. Repeat for the opposite upper corner.

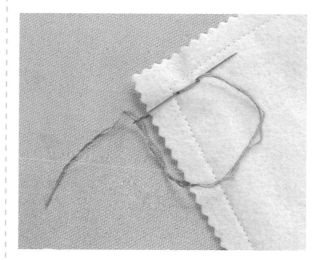

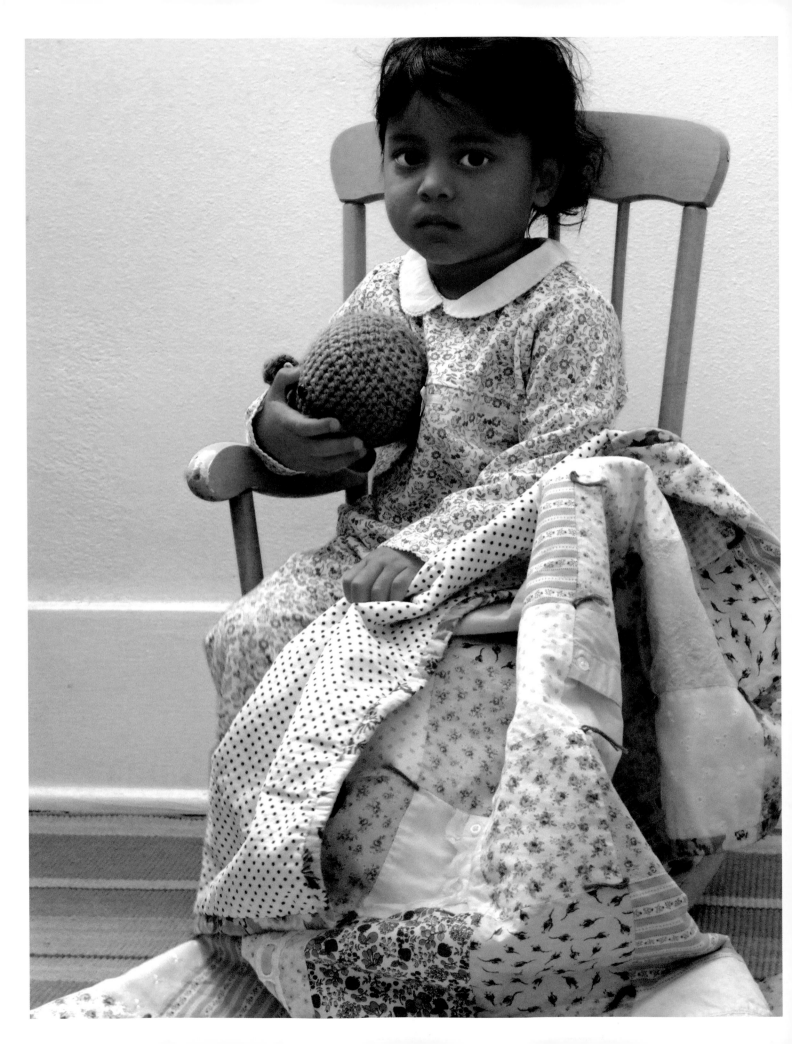

baby clothes quilt

The baby clothes quilt is a timeless classic, made by mothers, grandmas, and aunties for centuries, but every one I've seen is an original. With the sweet little tucks, pleats, buttons, and bows of your own baby's clothes, this quilt feels like a whole laundry basket of tiny treasures. The dressmaker details—plackets, smocking, yokes, trims—add charm and dimension, so just cut patches directly out of clothes that sport these intricate features. It's much lovelier to "save" clothes this way than to pack them in a box—destination: attic.

MATERIALS
For the quilt top: Eighty 5" x 5" (12.5cm x 12.5cm) squares of assorted cotton fabrics
For the quilt back: 1 3/8 yd (126cm) of 45"- (114cm-) wide cotton print
For the lining: 1 3/8 yd (126cm) of 45"- (114cm-) wide cotton batting

For the binding: 4 3/4 yd (5.2m) of 1" (2.5cm) double-fold binding
Rotary cutter
Self-healing cutting mat
Clear plastic ruler
80 medium-sized safety pins
Embroidery floss
Tape maker, 1" (2.5cm) size

FINISHED SIZE
36 1/2" x 45 1/2" (93cm x 116cm)
SEAM ALLOWANCE
1/4" (6mm), unless otherwise noted

1. First, if you are using pieces cut from baby clothes, stitch plackets or other open holes closed, and baste nonsquare pieces onto squares of plain cotton. Just pin each piece onto a square, with each right side up, and stitch close to the edge around all sides, securing the clothing piece evenly.

2. With the right sides of the squares together, stitch all the squares into strips of 10. You should have 8 long strips. Press all seams open.

3. Lay out the 8 strips, right side up and parallel, on a flat surface until the arrangement pleases you. Then, starting at one end, pin (with straight pins) 2 strips together, right sides facing and seams matching. Stitch down the length. Repeat for each strip, adding each new strip to the ever-growing quilt top, one after another. Press all seams open.

4. To make the quilt "sandwich," lay the backing fabric right side down on a flat surface. Lay the batting piece smoothly on top of the quilt back piece. Lay the quilt top right side up on top of the stack. (The quilt top will be smaller than the batting lining and the quilt back.) Starting in the center of the quilt, pin a safety pin through the center of each square, pinning all 3 layers together smoothly.

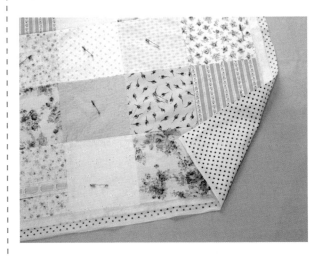

5. Baste the 3 layers of the quilt together around all 4 edges. Trim the excess batting and backing, making sure all your edges are straight. Following instructions in General Sewing Techniques (page 125), make and then apply binding around the entire edge of the quilt by machine and by hand.

6. Thread a sharp needle with a long length of embroidery floss. At each four-patch intersection, insert the needle through the front of the quilt and make a $1/8$" (3mm) stitch, leaving two 3" (7.5cm) tails coming up through the front of the quilt. Tie the tails into a knot and trim to about 1" (2.5cm). Wash and dry the quilt. Remove from the dryer and cuddle happily.

TIPS:

* Cutting your squares exactly square helps tremendously when making a simple quilt like this one. I myself wouldn't do this project without a rotary cutter, a clear ruler, and a self-healing cutting mat. If you invest in these tools, they'll pay you back a thousandfold.

* If you don't have enough baby clothes waiting to be turned into patches, simply supplement your squares with complementary new fabrics; a mix of old and new is just fine. Don't wash your new fabrics before making the quilt; you'll wash and dry the finished quilt. It's so satisfying to pull the rumpled, puckered quilt out of a hot dryer the first time—all your little mistakes will be invisible.

* For me, when sewing squares together, "random" patches of fabric truly means random. I reach for patches willy-nilly when sewing my first long strips. Then when I'm done making all the strips, I lay them out to ensure that I have a nice balance and that not too many of the same print or color are touching each other. You can plan the whole thing by laying out your squares and picking them up in rows, but I like the spontaneous effect of two squares of the same print winding up next to each other.

It's amazing how kids change without our really noticing sometimes. They seem to grow up fast, but in a day-to-day way, the changes are subtle. Ticking off the inches on a growth chart is a time-honored tradition that is often tracked in pencil on a doorjamb, only to be lost when the family moves (or repaints!). Shaped like a tall, multistory townhouse, this portable, fabric-based growth chart can witness both the years and changes of room or residence. Mark your child's name and measuring date on the chart with a fine-tip permanent marker. You can just roll up the growth chart when it's time to store it away.

MATERIALS

Townhouse Growth Chart templates (page 148)

For first floor of townhouse: One 10" x 7 1/2" (25.5cm x 19cm) piece of cotton print

For upper floors: Six 10" x 3 1/2" (25.5cm x 9cm) pieces each of 2 different cottons

For roof center: One 4 1/2" x 5 3/4" (11.5cm x 14.5cm) piece of striped cotton

For roof sides: One roughly 12" x 12" (30.5cm x 30.5cm) piece of striped cotton

For door: One 9" x 6" (23cm x 15cm) piece of cotton print

For window frame: One 3 3/4" x 4 3/4" (9.5cm x 11.5cm) pieces of cotton print

For windowpane: One 4 1/2" x 5 1/2" (11.5cm x 14cm) piece of white cotton

For felt backing: 12" x 51" (30.5 x 130cm) piece of wool felt

For binding: 3 1/2 yd (3.2m) of purchased 1/2" (13mm) double-fold binding

Rotary cutter

Self-healing cutting mat

Embroidery floss

4" (10cm) embroidery hoop

2"- (5cm-) wide clear plastic ruler

Purchased tape measure

Scotch tape

2 sets of small eyelets

Eyelet tool

FINISHED SIZE

10" x 49" (25.5cm x 125cm)

SEAM ALLOWANCE

1/4" (6mm), unless otherwise noted

1. To make the first floor, turn under a 1/4" (6mm) hem on the sides and the top of the door piece. With the right side up and bottom edges even, pin the door to the right side of the first floor piece and topstitch around the edge of the door to attach. Embroider the door details with 3 strands of embroidery floss and backstitches, per photo (see Embroidery [page 134]).

2. To make the roof, trace 2 Townhouse Side Roof template pieces (flip template over to trace second piece) onto the wrong side of fabric, cutting them on the bias. With right sides together, machine-sew the roof side pieces to the roof center piece. Press the seams toward the sides.

3. To make the window appliqué, turn under a 1/4" (6mm) hem on all sides of the frame piece. Trace the Townhouse Windowpane template onto the wrong side of the windowpane fabric. Cut out the windowpane and press in 1/4" (6mm) on each side. Pin the windowpane to the window frame and topstitch around the edge of the pane to attach. Then pin and topstitch the finished window piece to the center of the roof piece. Embroider the windowpane lines with 3 strands of embroidery

floss in a back stitch, per photo (see Embroidery [page 134]).

4. To make the upper 12 floors, lay 2 of the contrasting pieces together with the right sides facing and stitch the long edge. Repeat this step for the other 11 stories, using alternating prints, to create one tall strip of 12 pieces. Press the seams open.

5. Lay the tape measure down the length of the upper floors strip, 2" (5cm) from the left edge, using the portion between the marks for 25" (63.5cm) and 60" (152.5cm). Cut off the ends of the tape measure. Secure the tape measure to the fabric with a few pieces of Scotch tape. Topstitch down each side of the tape, using thread to match the color of the tape measure and sewing through the Scotch tape. Remove the Scotch tape.

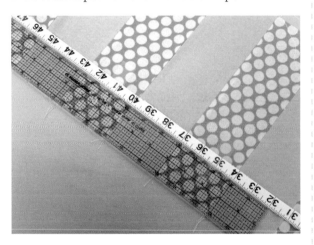

6. With the right side of the first floor facing the right side of the first strip of the upper floors, stitch the pieces together. With the right sides together, stitch the roof to the top of the upper floors strip. Press the seams open.

7. Lay the townhouse right side up on the piece of wool felt. Pin the two layers together and baste them together close to the outside edge of the townhouse. (You will have some extra felt here just to make it easier to keep things smooth when

stitching pieces together.) Trim extra felt and fabric from the edges, leaving a $1/8$" (3mm) seam allowance. Apply binding by machine and by hand around the outside edge of the townhouse (see General Sewing Techniques [page 125]).

8. Place the 2 eyelets in the upper corners of the roof, following the manufacturer's instructions for your eyelet tool.

TIP:
* When you're choosing fabrics, keep in mind that you'll be writing on the growth chart with a fine-tip permanent marker. You'll want to select prints that are subtle enough that individual names and dates will be easily read.

memory game

So often we take photos of people and forget about what's in the background. But what's in the background—the wallpaper, the pets, the furniture—says a lot about who we are and were, and can evoke memories as strongly as any song or smell. The classic memory game of Concentration—where you lay all tiles facedown, then flip photos one at a time, searching for pairs—is updated here with eighteen of your own family's photos from daily life, preserving familiar sights long after the background has changed.

MATERIALS

18 photos, sized at 2 1/2" x 2 1/2" (6.5cm x 6.5cm) and 200 dpi
For tile tops: Six 8 1/2" x 11" (21.5cm x 28cm) sheets of ink-jet printer–ready white fabric

For tile linings: Seventy-two 4" x 4" (10cm x 10cm) pieces of wool felt (about 1 yd [91cm] of 36"- [91cm-] wide fabric) in a light color
For tile backings: Thirty-six 4" x 4" (10cm x 10cm) pieces of cotton prints (about 3/8 yd [34.5cm] of 45"- [114cm-] wide fabric)

Rotary cutter
Self-healing cutting mat
Clear plastic ruler
Acid-free glue stick
Zigzag pinking shears

FINISHED SIZE

Thirty-six 3" x 3" (7.5cm x 7.5cm) tiles

1. To make the tops of the 36 tiles, create six 8 1/2" x 11" (21.5cm x 28cm) documents in any image-editing program. Then paste 6 images—2 copies of each photo—into each document, keeping a 1/2" (13mm) border of white space around each image. You will have 36 images total—2 copies of each of 18 different photos—when you're ready to print. Print out a test page on paper, then print all images onto the fabric sheets (see Transferring Photos to Fabric [page 133]). Using a rotary cutter, self-healing cutting mat, and ruler, trim each image into a 3" (7.5cm) square, keeping a 1/4" (6mm) white border around the sides of each photo.

2. To make a tile, stack the fabric layers as follows: On the bottom, place the cotton print, right side down. Then place 2 layers of wool felt. Then place the photo fabric, image side up, centered on the

stack. Put a small dab of glue between each layer to hold all 4 pieces together without pinning (a pin might leave a hole in the photo fabric layer).

3. The bottom layers are a bit larger than the photo fabric so that it's easier to keep all layers lined up. Machine-sew through the tile layers around the outline of the photo, backstitching to secure. When stitching, begin and end at a point on the image where the thread color matches the photo color, for the least noticeable join.

4. Trim the edge of the tile with pinking shears, leaving a narrow white border around the image.

TIP:

★ This project would also be an ideal one to do with photos of long-distance relatives the kids don't see frequently, or vacation photos from a favorite trip. You can adjust the number of total tiles to any even square number. Just remember that the number of total tiles should be *double* the number of images you use.

superhero cape

This idea came from my friend Sarah, who made something similar for her kids when they wanted to play dress up. The morning I stopped by to see their capes, they were zooming around in them so proudly I could hardly get a look—superhero powers activated! This cape is designed in two sizes— the smaller cape works for toddlers like Charlotte, and the larger (which is longer) is good for Oliver-sized kiddos (about age five).

MATERIALS

For small cape: 1/2 yd (45.5cm) of 45"-(114cm-) wide cotton

For the large cape: 2/3 yd (61cm) of 45"- (114cm-) wide cotton

For the small lining: 1/2 yd (45.5cm) of 45"- (114cm-) wide cotton

For the large lining: 2/3 yd (61cm) of 45"- (114cm-) wide cotton

For the monogram: One 8 1/2" x 11" (21.5cm x 28cm) piece of cotton

For the tie: 1 yd (91cm) of 1"- (2.5cm-) wide double-fold binding

For each row of trim: 1 yd (91cm) of rickrack, pom-poms, lace, or other trims of your choice

Pencil

String or yarn

Double-sided fusible web (like Heat 'n' Bond)

Tape maker, 1" (2.5cm) size

FINISHED SIZE

Small cape, about 13" (33cm) from neck edge to bottom; large cape, about 19" (48.5cm) from neck edge to bottom

SEAM ALLOWANCE

1/4" (13mm)

1. To make the cape (which is shaped like a quarter-circle), stack the cape fabric and the lining fabric, wrong sides together, with the edges even. To mark the curved lines, tie a string to a pencil. To make the neckline, knot the string 2 1/2" (6.5cm) from the pencil. Place the knot at one of the top corners of the stack of fabric. Hold down the knot while dragging the pencil in a smooth curve across the fabric to trace the neckline of the cape. To make the hemline, knot the string 16" (40.5cm) from the pencil for the small cape, and 22" (56cm) from the pencil for the large cape. Place the knot at the same corner of the fabric and trace the hemline. Keeping the 2 layers together, cut out the cape and lining pieces on the marked lines.

2. Following manufacturer's instructions, iron the double-sided fusible web, paper side up, onto the wrong side of the monogram fabric, leaving the paper in place. To make the monogram, using your computer, choose an easy-to-read font for your child's initial, and print out the initial so that it is about 8" (20.5cm) tall. Cut the initial from the paper and trace it, wrong side down, onto the paper backing of the fusible web (now fused to the fabric). Cut it out with the paper backing in place. Then remove the paper backing and place the initial, right side up, in the center back of the cape, and, following the manufacturer's instructions, press it to secure it to the cape piece. Machine-sew with a small, tight zigzag stitch around the entire edge of the initial.

3. To apply the trim, pin each trim smoothly in rows along the bottom of the cape. Machine-sew, securing well. If you want rickrack to hang down from the bottom edge, center and baste it along the seamline, making sure that upward-facing points

won't be caught in the side seamline (see the next step).

4. Place the cape and the lining pieces with right sides together, and pin around all edges. Stitch around the cape, leaving the neck open. Turn the cape right side out through the neck opening, and press flat.

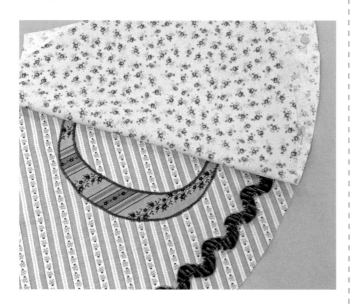

TIPS:
* Take your kids to the fabric store with you and let them pick out fabrics and trims to personalize their own capes. This is a fun project where you can really go crazy with the details— add as many rows of trim as you (they!) want.

* The monogram appliqué is attached to the cape using double-sided fusible web, and it and the trims are machine-sewed on, since this play costume will get a lot of wear.

5. Add pom-pom trim to the bottom edge by stitching it to the lining side of the cape (so poms hand down), tucking raw edges of trim under to finish. Pin ribbon on outside of cape to hide seamline, and machine-sew down both long edges.

6. To make the binding for the tie, follow the instructions in General Sewing Techniques (page 125). Fold the cut ends of the tape under $1/2$" (13mm) to finish them. Then mark the center of the length of tape. Place the center of the tape at the center back of the neck opening, and enclose the neck edge with the tape. Pin the tape in place. Then stitch down one end of the folded tape (backstitching to finish), then along the entire length, catching the neckline in the stitching, and then up the opposite end, backstitching to finish.

kid's drawing softie

My niece is a horse girl, as I was. I hold my breath when I watch her draw, remembering my own adventures in equine portraiture. I asked her to draw a colorful side view of a horse for me when I wanted to create this softie. I wish I had a picture of her face when she saw Megan (what I named the softie) sitting on my bed one day. Her smile bloomed with pure wonder as she recognized her drawing in its new, three-dimensional incarnation.

You can make the horsie from my template, or create a similar critter from any quadruped your child dreams up, since the basic principle for creating a gusset applies. It would be adorable to do one in the shape and colors of the family dog or cat, since children are usually well-practiced in drawing these familiar companions. But crazy colors work, too— the more creative they are, the more fun you'll have.

MATERIALS
Kid's Drawing Softie template (page 149), or child's drawing of a 4-legged animal

For the body: ¹/₂ yd (45.5cm) wool felt
For the markings: Scraps of wool felt in assorted colors
For the mane and tail: 3 yd (2.75m) of sportweight yarn

Medium-tip black marker
Embroidery floss in assorted colors
Wool batting or fiberfill for stuffing

FINISHED SIZE
About 13" x 9" (33cm x 23cm)

1. Make a photocopy of your child's drawing, or make 3 copies of the Horse and Ear templates (page 149). If you're using your child's drawing, on the copy, outline the animal with the black marker, simplifying the details so the critter has 2 legs, and eliminating the ears, mane, and tail (keep a dog or cat tail intact). Trace this simplified outline onto a clean sheet of paper, and enlarge it to the desired size on a copier. Make 3 copies of the enlarged pattern.

2. For one copy of the pattern, cut out the body of the animal. With the second copy, cut out all the markings. With the third copy, draw a line from the middle of the chest (point A), down and around the front leg, along the belly, down and around the back leg, and up to the middle rear of the animal

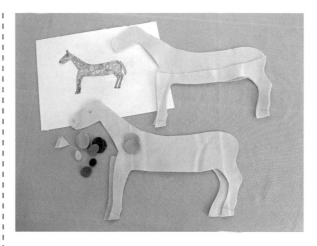

(point B), then across the body back to point A. For a dog or a cat, point B is just below the tail. Cut out the lower half of the animal along this line. This piece will be a gusset.

3. From the felt for the body, cut 2 complete bodies and 2 bottom gussets. Do not add seam allowances. From the scraps of felt for the markings, cut 2 copies of each marking. Attach the markings to the 2 body pieces with 2 strands of embroidery floss, using a blanket stitch (see Hand-Sewing [page 130]).

4. With the wrong sides together, sew one bottom gusset to each body piece around the legs and bottom of the body, using 2 strands of embroidery floss in a blanket stitch (leave the straight [belly] edge of the gusset open). With the wrong sides together, blanket stitch the 2 body pieces together from point A (the chest), around the head and across the back, to point B (the back of the legs), leaving the gusset open.

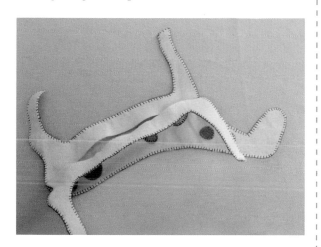

5. Stuff the body with batting or fiberfill (a hemostat or toy-stuffing tool can help here; see Resources [page 143]), and sew the gusset opening closed with a blanket stitch. Using a few whipstitches (see Hand-Sewing [page 130]) in thread the same color as the body, tack each inner back thigh to the belly (this will pull the legs in so the critter can stand on all 4 legs).

6. Embroider the features of the face with 2 strands of embroidery floss, using a knotless start (see Hand-Sewing [page 130]).

7. For ears, cut 2 small triangles of felt or follow the Ear template. For stand-up ears, fold the triangles in half lengthwise and tack them to the sides of the head. For floppy ears, tack the short edge of the triangle flat against the side of the head, so the tip of the ear hangs down.

8. To make the mane and forelock (for a horse), cut twenty-six 3" (7.5cm) strands of the yarn. For the mane, sew the first strand (of 22) through the seam on the top of the head at the ears, centering the strand so half falls on each side of the head. Repeat along the back of the neck with the other 21 pieces of the mane. For the forelock, repeat with the remaining 4 strands, moving across the head from one ear to the other, and trim to forelock length.

9. For the tail, cut three 8" (20.5cm) strands of yarn. Sew them onto the rear of the horse above point B, centering the 3 strands.

TIP:

* Simplifying your child's drawing will make it easier to create a pattern for it. I traced my niece's horse and used the facing legs to create a template for all four legs. You can simplify features like spots, mane, and tail while still maintaining the spirit of the drawing. I stitched the facial features after the animal was stuffed, which gave me more control when trying to capture Megan's expression ("pleasantly optimistic").

sleepover pillowcase

A first sleepover away from home is a big deal (especially for Mom and Dad)! If your sleepover-goer gets nervous, a phone number nearby can calm any potential homesickness. I've made this pillowcase out of silky-smooth cotton lawn, but you could use any soft cotton calico. It's great if you can find rickrack that comes in a couple of different sizes to coordinate the hem and the telephone number, but the hem could also be trimmed with ribbon, pom-poms, or any whimsical edging your child might like.

MATERIALS

For pillowcase: One 28" x 43" (71cm x 109cm) piece of printed cotton lawn

For hem: One 11" x 43" (28cm x 109cm) piece of solid cotton

For hem trim: 1¼ yd (114cm) of 1"- (2.5cm-) wide rickrack

For numbers: 1¾ yd (1.6m) of ½"- (13mm-) wide rickrack

Clear plastic ruler

Fabric marker

Embroidery floss in same color as small rickrack

4" (10cm) embroidery hoop

Zigzag pinking shears

FINISHED SIZE

32" x 21" (81cm x 53.5cm)

SEAM ALLOWANCE

½" (13mm), unless otherwise noted

1. To make the hem, fold and press the hem piece lengthwise, then again crosswise to create 4 quadrants. Unfold the hem piece. Along one long edge of the piece (the top), press under 3/4" (2cm). On the bottom edge, press under 1/2" (13mm).

2. To prepare the phone number, using your computer, find a font that will give you clear, simple digits (I used Arial at 210-point size). Size your phone number so the individual numbers are about 2" (5cm) high and the entire phone number is about 14" (35.5cm) long. Lay out the number on 2 separate lines on the page, print it, and then cut it into 2 pieces and tape them together, making sure to align the pieces so the telephone number is straight. Center the phone number design beneath the fabric of the upper-left quadrant of the hem piece, using the pressed lines and a clear ruler to guide you. Trace the number with a fabric marker. (If you're using a dark fabric, you might want to use the carbon-transfer method, but these numbers are big, so you should be able to see them through the fabric.)

3. To make the phone number, cut the length of small rickrack into pieces, one piece per digit. (Make sure you have a bit more per digit than you think you need.) Place the embroidery hoop on the hem piece around the first traced number. Tucking the cut ends of the rickrack under and using 2 strands of embroidery floss, tack the rickrack into numerals with tiny stitches at each point. Move the hoop along the hem piece to tack the rickrack of each number, being careful not to scrunch the rickrack from previous numbers with the hoop. Press the hem piece when finished.

4. To attach the hem piece to the pillowcase piece, lay the pillowcase piece right side up. Lay the large rickrack along a long edge of the pillowcase piece, with the center of the trim 1/2" (13mm) away from raw edge. Open out the hem piece and, with the top edge pressed under, pin, right side up along the long edge of the pillowcase piece, overlapping the raw edge of the pillowcase piece 1/2" (13mm) and allowing the top edges of the rickrack to peek out (see photo). Baste 1/4" (6mm) from the folded (top) edge of the hem.

5. Fold the pillowcase in half lengthwise, with right sides together and the hem opened out. Stitch along the side and the length of the pillowcase and hem. Trim the edges of the seam allowances with

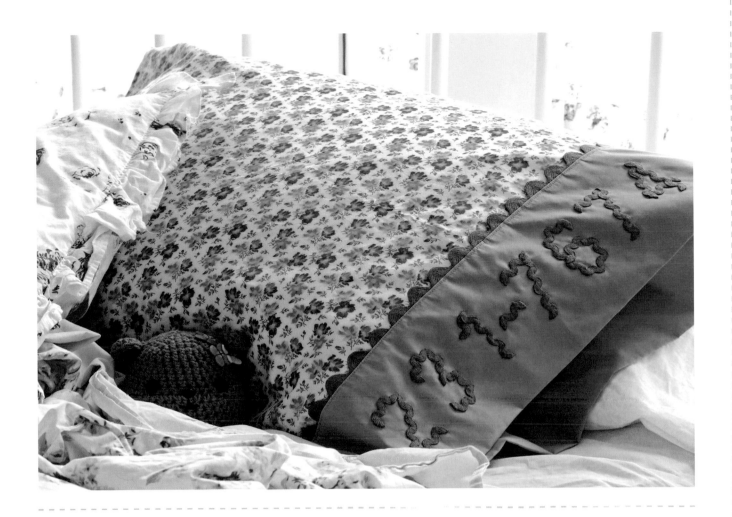

pinking shears. (If you have an overlock stitch on your machine, you can finish the edges that way.)

6. Turn the pillowcase right side out and fold the hem to the inside along the hem's lengthwise fold line, keeping the bottom edge turned under. Pin along the basting stitches, securing the turned-under edge on the wrong side. On the right side, topstitch close to the edge of the hem, being sure to catch the interior turned-under hem in the seam. Remove the pins and basting. Press.

TIPS:

* For sizing the phone number, any simple sans-serif font will work. I used a common font called Arial and sized it to 210 points. When centering the phone number on the hem, leave enough space between the numbers to fit the rickrack and allow a nice margin.

* When topstitching the hem, catching the hem on both the outside and the inside can be tricky. Use plenty of pins, go slowly to avoid puckers, and check the inside often. Use the sleeve arm on your sewing machine so the fabric can loop easily.

PART TWO:

FOR
EVERY DAY

At our house, we're all about the everyday stuff. We like the regular, the routine, the quotidian. We like the hanging-out with pizza and beer, the couch party with a cat on a lap, the movie nights with movies we've seen seven times already and friends who don't (seem to) mind.

We like the averageness of the nothin'-doin', no-fuss day. Those unspecial days are, in my opinion, actually the most special. When times are complicated, those days are the ones that I appreciate most of all, and long to have back.

But just because I go through most of those days wearing nothing fancier than jeans (okay, sweatpants) and there's nobody here but my hubby (okay, my puppy) to help me celebrate, celebrate the everyday I do. I take pictures every day, of everything: my breakfast, my pets, my yarn, my flower, my pumpkin, my family, my porch light, my pillow, my heart-shaped biscuit flecked with parsley on its bed of chicken stew. I photograph everything. It's really not that hard. You just pick up your camera and point it at something. Then pick it up again, and point it at something else tomorrow. If you start a blog, you can put the picture up there. Then you can blather on about it, telling half the world that you had cloudberry jam on toast for breakfast. You wouldn't think anyone would care. But for some weird reason they do. They had cloudberry jam yesterday, too, or will tomorrow. You thought you were the only one? No. We're all in this together.

The best thing about having a blog is that, if you do it every day, you start to see every day as an opportunity, not just to take a picture of and talk about jam, but to look at things differently.

An opportunity to gain some perspective on the prosaic aspects of our lives, those we tend to take for granted. If life has ever thrown you a few lemons, and you've found yourself longing for the luxury of an unremarkable Tuesday, then you know just what I mean. I think sewing things that celebrate the Tuesdays, the cloudberry-jam days, and the nothin'-doin' days makes them special days, after all.

The projects in this section were designed to celebrate the laundry, the dinner, and the people and pets in your pack in all their wonderful averageness. They are not meant to be precious but to be used well, on an everyday basis. Some, like the First Apartment Laundry Bag and Felted Sweater Bag, are made of fabrics that are special because they have already been well-loved by you or yours. Other projects, like the Family Recipe Book, commemorate the everyday mealtimes of the past, present, and future by giving you a special place to keep your family's favorites. Whichever ones you choose to complete, these projects help you celebrate the everyday, with things you'll use every day.

◄ *Chicken stew and heart-shaped biscuits sit so patiently for their portrait.*

family photo pillow

There is such a classic quality to old photos, and I think it has a lot to do with the formal feel of black-and-white film. When the images are cropped to include just the faces, the trappings of time and place tend to disappear, and all the similarities rise to the surface: Your daughter looks like your Aunt Grace and no one's ever noticed. This pillow features sixteen fabric patches printed with the beautiful faces of family members, from grandparents to nieces and nephews. I made these patches with all the immediate members of my husband's and my families, and I think it would make a fantastic wedding present for newlyweds who've recently merged their clans.

MATERIALS

16 photos, sized at 4 3/4" x 4 3/4" (12cm x 12cm) and 200 dpi

For photo patches: 8 sheets of ink-jet printer–ready white fabric

For pillow back: Two 14" x 17 1/2" (35.5cm x 44.5cm) pieces of cotton print

For the trim: 2 1/2 yd (2.3m) of piping trim

Pillow form: 18" x 18" (45.5cm x 45.5cm)

Rotary cutter

Self-healing cutting mat

Clear plastic ruler

FINISHED SIZE

To fit an 18" (45.5cm) square pillow form

SEAM ALLOWANCE

1/4" (6mm), unless otherwise noted

1. To make the photo patches, print the photos onto the fabric sheets, 2 per sheet, following the directions in Transferring Photos to Fabric (page 133). Remember that there is a 1/4" (6mm) seam allowance built into this square; when centering the person's face, be sure to leave a margin so you don't chop off somebody's chin! Cut out each photo around the printed area.

2. Arrange the squares in a pleasing way. With the right sides of the squares together, stitch all the squares into strips of 4. You should end up with 4 strips of 4 images each. Press all seams open. Lay out the strips, right side up and parallel. Then, starting at one end, pin 2 strips together, right sides facing and seams aligned. Stitch down the length. Repeat for each strip,

adding each new strip to the pillow top, one after another. Press all seams open.

3. Pin the piping trim around the outside edge of the pillow top, raw edges even and clipping piping seam allowance almost to piping at corners to turn sharply. Machine-baste the trim to the top using a scant 1/4" (6mm) seam.

4. For the pillow back piece, on one back piece turn under 1" (2.5cm) on the long edge and press; turn under 1" (2.5cm) again and press. Topstitch along each edge of the hem. Repeat for the other back piece.

5. With the right side up, lay the pillow front (with the basted trim in place) flat on the work surface. Lay the 2 back pieces right side down on top of the

pillow front, overlapping the hemmed edges. Pin all thicknesses together around the edges.

6. Machine-sew using a $^1/_4$" (6mm) seam around the pillowcase, pivoting at the corners. Be careful not to catch the piping in the stitching (just the seam allowance). Clip the corners, turn the pillow cover right side out, and press. Stuff with the pillow form.

TIPS:

* If you want to scan old photos, make sure to scan them at a high resolution (like 300 dpi or higher, depending on how large your originals are) so that you will have plenty of pixels when resizing.

* Place the photos in a random order, based on size and content of image, not family relationship: big faces next to small faces, couples next to singles, and both sides of the family well-mixed in the arrangement.

I designed this laundry bag while thinking about leaving home for the first time, and the new activities—like doing your own laundry—that are traditional rites of passage. "Souvenirs" from Dad's and a brother's closets— the pleated strips that decorate the bottom half of the bag are made from men's shirts and shirting fabrics—are little pieces of home away from home, or "laundry away from Mom's laundry room."

MATERIALS

For bag front bottom and top and bag back bottom and top: Four 19" x 15" (48.5cm x 38cm) pieces of canvas ticking

For lining: Two 19" x 28" (48.5cm x 71cm) pieces of checked gingham

For pleated strips: Eight pairs of 20" x 4" (51cm x 10cm) pieces of assorted shirting fabrics

For drawstring: 1 1/2 yd (1.4m) of 1/4"- (6mm-) cording

Rotary cutter

Self-healing cutting mat

Clear plastic ruler

Zigzag pinking shears

FINISHED SIZE

18" x 27" (45.5cm x 68cm)

SEAM ALLOWANCE

1/2" (13mm), unless otherwise noted

1. To prepare the pleated strips, fold each strip in half lengthwise, wrong sides together, and press. Lay one strip horizontally across the bag front bottom piece with the folded edge of the strip exactly 6" (15cm) from the bottom edge (and the raw edge toward the top of the bag piece). Fold a 1/2" (13mm) pleat into the strip anywhere along the length (the length of the strip will then be the same as the width as the bag piece). Pin along the upper edges of the strip. Using a zigzag stitch, sew the top of the strip to the front of the bag piece, catching the raw edges of the strip to prevent fraying.

2. Lay the next strip horizontally across the bag front bottom piece, with the folded edge exactly 1" (2.5cm) above the folded edge of the previous strip. Fold a 1/2" (13mm) pleat into the strip at a different location than the pleat below. Using a zigzag stitch, sew the strip to the bag piece. Repeat for the remaining 6 strips, making sure that the

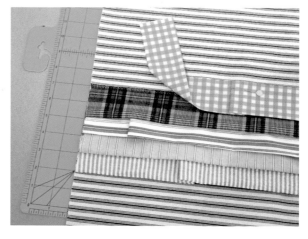

last strip lines up evenly with the top edge of the bag front bottom piece.

3. With the right sides together, place the front top piece over the front bottom piece with all edges even. Using a straight stitch, sew along the top edge, using a 1" (2.5cm) seam allowance. Trim the seam with pinking shears, and press it toward the top of the bag.

4. Repeat steps 1 through 3 to make the back of the bag.

5. On the wrong side of the front of the bag, mark a 1"- (2.5cm-) wide opening on one of the side seamlines 3" (7.5cm) from the top of the bag. With the right sides of the front and back bag pieces together and the marked piece facing up, sew the long (side) edges of the bag, backstitching on each side of the opening. Stitch along the bottom edge of the bag. Stitch across the bottom corners about 1 1/2" (3.8cm) from the edge to create a square bottom (see General Sewing Techniques [page 125]). Press the seams open and turn the bag right side out.

6. To make the lining, place the right sides of the front and back lining pieces together and stitch down the long edges. Stitch across the bottom of the lining, leaving an 8" (20.5cm) opening through which you will turn the bag. Stitch across the bottom corners about 1 1/2" (3.8cm) from the edge to create a square bottom (see General Sewing Techniques [page 125]).

7. With right sides together, place the outer bag into the lining (the wrong side of the lining will be facing you). With the top edges even, stitch around the top of the bag through both layers. Pull the outer bag through the opening in the lining. Turn in the edges of the lining and machine-sew the

opening closed. Turn the lining to the inside and press the top edge of the bag.

8. To make the drawstring casing, find the opening in the side seam. With the outside of the bag facing you, at the ends of the opening, stitch 2 rows of straight stitches parallel to each other (and to the top of the bag) through both layers of fabric, 1" (2.5cm) apart.

9. To run the drawstring through the casing, attach a large safety pin to one end of the cord. Feed the cord through the casing around the circumference of the bag. Leave about 6" (15cm) of extra cord, and tie the ends into a strong knot. Feed the knot back into the casing so it is hidden.

new home place mats

I'm a huge fan of housewarming gifts. For a long time I gave handknit dishcloths and organic cleaning supplies to my friends when they moved into new digs, but I really like the idea of creating something permanent to commemorate such an exciting life change. These linen place mats feature an appliqué of a photo of the new house along with the new address printed directly on a piece of twill tape you send through your ink-jet printer. They'd be perfect as a hostess gift for the first of many dinner parties. You may just get invited back.

MATERIALS FOR 2 PLACE MATS
One photo, sized at 4" x 3" (10cm x 7.5cm) and 200 dpi
For photo patches: One 8 1/2" x 11" (21.5cm x 28cm) piece of cream-colored linen
For place mats: Four 18" x 13 1/2" (45.5cm x 34.5cm) pieces of linen
For interlining: Two 18" x 13 1/2" (45.5cm x 34.5cm) pieces of Timtex or other heavyweight, sew-in stabilizer

For trim: 3 3/4 yd (4.1m) of 1" (2.5cm) double-fold binding
For address label: 1 yd (91cm) of cream-colored 1/2"- (13mm-) wide twill tape
One 8 1/2" x 11" (21.5cm x 28cm) piece of full-sheet sticker paper
Embroidery floss
Tape maker, 1" (2.5cm) size
Bubble-jet setter
Rotary cutter

Self-healing cutting mat
Clear plastic ruler
Double-sided tape
FINISHED SIZE
18" x 13 1/2" (45.5cm x 34.5cm)
SEAM ALLOWANCE
1/4" (6mm), unless otherwise noted

1. To prepare your photo fabric and twill tape, treat both according to the bubble-jet setter manufacturer's instructions. To prepare your photo, on your computer crop your image in a pleasing way to be approximately 4" x 3" (10cm x 7.5cm) at 200 dpi. (Exact size is not super important for the image, so if it looks best cropped to slightly different dimensions, go for it. You want it to be big enough to reveal details of the house but not so big that it looks disproportionate to the place mat.) Place 2 copies of the image on one page, leaving at least 1/2" (13mm) around all sides of each. Smooth the full sheet of sticker paper onto the wrong side of the piece of cream-colored linen. Print the photos onto the linen piece, using your ink-jet printer (see Transferring Photos to Fabric [page 133]). Rinse the linen fabric until water runs clear, then dry and press with a warm iron to heat-set the image.

2. Trim each photo, leaving a 1/2" (13mm) border on all sides. Press under a 1/4" (6mm) hem on all sides. Pin the photo appliqué to the bottom right corner of the place mat top piece, and attach by sewing with slip stitches (see Hand-Sewing [page 130]), leaving about 1 1/2" (3.8cm) of space between the edge of the appliqué and the bottom and the side edges of the place mat. Repeat for the second place mat.

3. To make the address label, on your computer create a document with a "landscape" orientation

(so your type will run horizontally across the wide measurement of a letter-size piece of paper). Type the address using a font that is easily readable and a size slightly smaller than $1/2$" (13mm) high. Print the address onto a sheet of regular paper. Using double-sided tape, attach a length of twill tape (keep it several inches [about 8cm] longer on each side of the address) to the paper, directly over the text you've printed. (You can also add a piece of Scotch tape to the end of the twill tape that will go through the printer first, to secure it.) Feed the paper into the printer so that the text will reprint in the same position. Print the address again. Remove the Scotch tape, and rinse the twill tape under running water, dry, and press to heat-set. Fold under the edges of the tape and, using 2 strands of embroidery floss, tack the address label to the place mat under the photo with a few straight stitches done by hand. Repeat for the second place mat.

4. Sandwich the Timtex between the place mat top and the other piece of linen for the back. Baste around the edge of the place mat through the 3 layers, a scant $1/4$" (6mm) from the edge. Repeat for the second place mat.

5. Following the instructions in General Sewing Techniques, make and apply the binding around the entire edge of the place mat by machine and by hand. Repeat for the second place mat.

TIPS:

* Photograph the house so that you crop out anything that interferes with an ideal impression. I used photo-editing software to take out some hanging leaves and telephone wires, and cropped the foreground to focus on the front entrance. Go for romantic rather than realistic.

* Timtex is a heavyweight stabilizer available at fabric stores. It's flexible and washable, yet stiff enough to give a lot of body to whatever it's lining. I prefer my place mats to be hefty; if you don't, just choose a lighter-weight, sew-in stabilizer.

* I printed my photo onto a small piece of cream-colored treated linen from my stash instead of on an ink-jet printer-ready fabric sheet (see Transferring Photos to Fabric [page 133]). Using fabric with a coarser weave results in a faded quality I like. Experiment with different fabrics until you get the look you prefer.

Warning: This is a cautionary tale!

It's not about why you should make lovely, hand-stitched gifts about special moments for the people you love. It's not about how you should wrap those gifts in beautiful paper with hand-stamped gift tags. It's about why you *shouldn't*.

Oh, not really. Don't worry. You'll see.

The thing about making handmade gifts and giving them to people you love is that sometimes *you* love what you've made more than they will.

Unless you've involved them in the process, it's occasionally inevitable that you'll like it more than they will. Even when you really tried to pick the things you think they'll love.

I think everyone who likes to make things has been there: You spend half the year—twenty-six lunch hours, fifteen Saturday nights, and seven fourth-grade soccer games, to be exact—secretly knitting your husband a sweater. You think of him wearing it on Sunday mornings while flipping pancakes, you picture how cool he'll

look in it while he walks through the park with the dog. You wrap it lovingly, then pass it to him excitedly—*Surely it must be the best birthday present the man has ever seen!*

And he says, "Oh—thanks . . . no, I like it!" Sigh.

But the thing about giving handmade gifts is that, as much as I want my recipient to love my present, to appreciate the hours I spent on it, and to think it's much better than the new iPod he'd been hinting about, I know I can't control what anyone's response will be when I give them what I've made. Sometimes they're thrilled, sincerely. Sometimes the initial reception is . . . less than thrilled, or thrilling.

It's really hard for people who don't sew (or knit, or quilt, or embroider, or crochet, or [insert name of time-consuming handwork here]) to be able to fully appreciate what goes into a handmade item. It's not that they don't love you, or don't care, or don't like it—I think sometimes it's that they might not understand it like you do. Especially kids. Not many kids are going to appreciate a handmade doll when what they really wanted was another [insert name of cool new must-have toy here].

But I think eventually they will. Given a little time—maybe a lot of time—I think it's always worth giving, and worth getting, handmade things. Even if the reaction we're hoping for is a bit delayed, or even invisible to us, there is no predicting that moment when someone is, perhaps years later, holding your precious gift in their hands and wishing they could do the moment over, or tell you now how much they appreciate your present.

The best present I ever made and gave was a set of embroidered, monogrammed pillowcases for my dad. It was his last Christmas with us, and only two weeks before he passed away. I'd picked a monogram for him in an Old English font that reminded me of him, and embroidered it in gray and silver floss on a set of pillowcases that were a beautiful pale blue, his favorite color. He wasn't able to talk well at that time. There were so many things I was unable to say. But I will never, ever forget his incredible smile as he opened it, and touched the stitches, and held a pillowcase up to see it better. I watched his face in amazement; I was shaky with love and hope. I think he understood then exactly what I'd needed to tell him, that there was no one else like him in the whole wide world.

His gift to me was that incredible smile. I've pulled it out of my memory and unwrapped it a thousand times since.

recipe-card apron

This project is one of my favorites. I love it for so many reasons, especially because of the cute little bird on the vintage recipe card. If you have a family recipe card with charming artwork, it's fun to pick up on the colors or style in the fabrics you use. Not to worry if you only have some handwritten notes from your grandma about her legendary cinnamon buns. This project is no less special. Taking inspiration from the cook who provided the recipe, choose fabrics she would've loved and worn. The cook's magic is sure to follow you into the kitchen every time you tie it on.

MATERIALS

Recipe card (to be horizontally oriented)

For pocket trim: One 10" (25cm) piece of $^1/_2$"- (13mm-) wide double-fold binding

For recipe-card pocket: One 8 $^1/_2$" x 11" (21.5cm x 28cm) sheet of ink-jet printer–ready fabric

For apron waistband: One 20" x 6" (51cm x 15cm) piece of 1" (2.5cm) gingham, cut on the bias (fabric A)

For apron ties: Two 30" x 4" (76cm x 10cm) pieces of fabric A, cut on straight grain

For apron front top panel: One 10" x 17" (25.5cm x 43cm) piece of cotton print (fabric B)

For apron side top panels: Two 10" x 17" (25.5cm x 43cm) pieces of cotton print (fabric C)

For apron front bottom panel: One 10" x 10" (25.5cm x 25.5cm) piece of fabric B

For apron side bottom panels: Two 10" x 10" (25.5cm x 25.5cm) pieces of fabric A, cut on the bias

For trim: 2 $^1/_2$ yd (1.8m) of $^1/_2$"- (13mm-) wide rickrack

Embroidery floss

FINISHED SIZE

About 19" x 22" (48.5cm x 56cm), with 29" (74cm) ties

SEAM ALLOWANCE

$^1/_4$" (6mm), unless otherwise noted

1. To make the recipe-card pocket, using the custom settings on your scanner, scan your recipe card at about 600 dpi. This setting will give you enough pixels to enlarge the recipe card image without losing quality. Don't worry too much about how tall the image is; the width is more important than the height. Print your recipe card image onto the ink-jet printer–ready fabric, and trim it into a rectangle 10" (25.5cm) wide, with about $^1/_2$" (13mm) of margin between the text and the edges of the fabric.

2. Following the directions in General Sewing Techniques (page 125), apply binding to the top edge of the pocket. Lay the pocket, right side up, on the right side of the front top panel with the bottoms and the edges of the pocket and panel aligned. Baste the pocket in place along the sides and the bottom edge.

3. Gather (see Hand-Sewing [Running Stitch, page 130]) the top edges of the side panels (fabric C) until they are about half their original width. With the right sides together, stitch the right and left side top panels to the front top panel (fabric B) along the long edges. Press the seams toward the front top panel. With the right sides together, stitch the right and left side bottom panels (fabric A) to the front bottom panel (fabric B) along the side edges. Press the seams toward the front bottom

• Here's what's cookin' **Apple Cake**   Serves 16

• Recipe from the kitchen of   mrs. Smrcka (Iowa)

4 cups apples

2 cups sugar

(Do not cook - let stand 1hr.)

Beat 2 eggs, adding

3/4 cup cooking oil and

1 tsp vanilla . Pour over apples.

mix together well:

2 cups all-purpose flour

1½ tsp baking soda

1 tsp salt

2 tsp cinnamon & 3/4 cup nuts.

panel. With the right sides together, pin the bottom panel piece to the top panel piece across the width of the apron. Stitch, and press the seams toward the bottom.

4. Lay the rickrack along the long seams between the panels. Tack at each point of the rickrack with small hand stitches, using 3 strands of contrasting embroidery floss. Hem the long edges of the side panels, turning under each edge $1/4$" (6mm) twice and stitching down the entire length. Then press under $1/2$" (13mm) along the bottom edge of the apron. Fold up the bottom of the apron to the back side so that the folded edge lies just above the seamline between the bottom panels and the top panels. Stitch, right side up, on top of this seamline again, catching the apron hem in the seam. Lay the rickrack along this seamline and tack with small hand stitches, turning under the raw ends of the rickrack to finish.

5. To make the waistband, press under $1/4$" (6mm) on the short edges. Fold the waistband piece (fabric A) in half lengthwise, with wrong sides together, then fold the long edges in again toward the fold, and press.

6. To make one apron tie, gather the short edge of the tie (fabric A), leaving that edge unfinished (you'll stick it into the waistband later). Hem the long edges and the remaining short edge, turning under each edge $1/4$" (6mm) twice and stitching. Turn the bottom corner of the short finished edge up to the back of the tie to make a 45-degree angle. Stitch across the top of the turned-under piece to hold the edge in place. Repeat for the second tie.

7. With the right side facing you, lay the top edge of the apron inside the folded waistband, making sure the waistband overlaps the apron by about $1/2$" (13mm), and pull up the gathers of the side panels so that the top edge of the apron is the same width as the waistband. Baste along the bottom edge of the waistband to hold it in place, making sure to catch both the front and the back sides in the stitches. Slide the gathered end of the ties into the side openings of the waistband, pulling up gathers to fit. Baste in place. Topstitch around the 3 edges of the waistband. Remove the basting stitches. Love it!

TIPS:

* Using checked gingham for the waistband, ties, and bottom panels is adorable and retro-y. If you want the squares to be diagonal, remember to purchase extra fabric, since those pieces will be cut on the bias. (The ties for this apron were actually cut on the straight grain; they are gathered, so the grain's not so obvious, and they use less fabric this way.)

* Stitching rickrack on by hand can be time-consuming, but I think it's very relaxing. If you don't agree, just zoom down each length of trim with a straight machine stitch.

friend chandelier

This project is a cool accessory for a freshman dorm room. Using photos of a teenager's friends, each "crystal" is lightly stuffed and set off by tiny fabric yo-yos. When grouped together, the shapes conjure a funky chandelier that keeps friends from home nearby. It works well for any group of friends— think summer-camp bunkmates, the volleyball team, or favorite sorority sisters. It would be adorable in school colors, too!

MATERIALS

Friend Chandelier template (page 150)
8 photos, sized at 3 1/2" x 4 1/2" (9cm x 11.5cm) and 200 dpi, with faces centered
For crystal fronts: Two 8 1/2" x 11" (21.5cm x 28cm) sheets of ink-jet printer–ready fabric sheets
For crystal backs: Eight 3 1/2" x 4 1/2" (9cm x 11.5cm) pieces of assorted cotton prints

For yo-yos: Sixteen 2 1/4"- (5.5cm-) diameter circles, cut from assorted cotton prints
For hanger: One 9" (23cm) inner ring of a wooden embroidery hoop
For ties: Two 36" (91cm) lengths of 3/8"- (9mm-) wide satin ribbon
1 1/8 yd (1.25cm) of 1/8"- (3mm-) wide leather lacing
One 8 1/2" x 11" (21.5cm x 28cm) piece of template plastic

Pearl cotton #5
Wool batting or polyester fiberfill
Heavyweight thread
Acrylic paint
Varnish
Paintbrush
4 small binder clips
Dressmaker's chalk
Fabric glue

1. To make the crystals, print the photos onto the fabric sheets, following the directions in Transferring Photos to Fabric (page 133). Grouping them in 2 rows of 2 on each sheet works well. Remember that you will be cutting the rectangular photos into the shape of a "crystal"; there is a 1/4" (6mm) seam allowance built into that shape. When centering the person's face, leave a margin so you don't wind up sewing someone's chin or cheeks into a seam allowance! Cut out each photo into a rectangular shape.

2. Trace the Crystal template onto the template plastic and cut it out. To make the crystal fronts, use dressmaker's chalk to trace the Crystal template onto the wrong side of every photo (crystal front), centering the face (you will be able to see the face through the fabric). With right

sides together, stitch one crystal front piece to one crystal back piece on the traced lines, leaving a bottom segment of the crystal open for stuffing. Trim around the seam, leaving a 1/8" (3mm) seam allowance. Clip the corners. Turn the crystal right side out. Use a blunt point, like a chopstick or crochet hook, to poke out the corners (don't push too hard or you'll poke through the seam). Stuff the crystal lightly with batting and slip stitch the openings closed. Repeat for the other 7 crystals.

3. To make the yo-yos, knot a 12" (30.5cm) length of heavyweight thread. Turn under a 1/4" (6mm) hem while making a row of running stitches around the edge of the circle. Pull the thread tight to create the yo-yo, and secure the thread with a few stitches at the beginning of the seam. (The

yo-yos will look like little flat pouches with a center hole where you have drawn up the thread (see General Sewing Techniques [page 125]). Repeat for the other 15 yo-yos. Set the yo-yos aside.

4. To string the crystals and yo-yos, with the pearl cotton, sew running stitches around the outside of one crystal $^1/8$" (3mm) from the edge, starting and ending at the bottom tip. Knot off but don't cut the pearl cotton. Thread one yo-yo onto the pearl cotton, running the pearl cotton through the diameter of the yo-yo and out the other side. Knot off and trim, leaving a $^1/4$" (6mm) tail. Thread an 18" (45.5cm) length of pearl cotton and attach it to the top of the crystal with a knot, burying the tail in the crystal. Thread another yo-yo onto the pearl cotton about 1" (2.5cm) from the top of the crystal, running the thread through the diameter of the yo-yo and out the other side. Knot off but do not trim the pearl cotton. Repeat for each crystal and pair of yo-yos to make 8 strings of shapes.

5. For the hanger, paint the embroidery hoop ring with 2 coats of acrylic paint, and let it dry. Apply one coat of varnish.

6. Wrap an end of one length of ribbon around the hoop, tucking in the raw edge. Glue the wrapped ribbon to the hoop, secure it with a binder clip, and let dry. On the opposite side of the hoop, repeat

with the other end of the length of ribbon. Repeat with the second length of ribbon, perpendicular to the first, so the ribbons are attached at equidistant quadrants on the hoop. Fold the middle sections of both ribbons to form a 4" (10cm) loop. Tie a 3" (7.5cm) length of leather lacing around the base of the loop (see photo).

7. Cut two 18" (45.5cm) lengths of leather lacing. Tie the lacing across the hoop, centering each end between the 2 ribbon ends and bowing the lacing slightly (see photo). Repeat with the other length of lacing, draping it slightly lower than the first. Tie one string of crystals and yo-yos to the leather cording (or to the hoop). Repeat for the other 7 strings of shapes. Adjust the lengths of the chandelier strings so they hang in a balanced way. Add a dab of glue to each knot, and trim the ends close to the knot.

farmgirl photo pillow

This pillow is a simple project that calls for a great photo from your collection, especially one that includes people you love. I took this photo one night while on a hayride with my friend Sarah and her family. The light of a midsummer evening and the intense colors of the sky, the farm in the background, and the gingham of Sarah's shirt inspired the fabrics I chose. Let the details of your photo suggest combinations for you.

MATERIALS

One photo, sized at 9" x 7" (23cm x 18cm) and 200 dpi.

For center patch (photo): One 8 1/2" x 11" (21.5cm x 28cm) sheet of ink-jet printer–ready white fabric

For top and bottom borders: Two 9" x 4" (23cm x 10cm) pieces of cotton print

For side borders: Two 3" x 14" (7.5cm x 35.5cm) pieces of cotton calico

For pillow back: Two 10" x 14" (25.5cm x 35.5cm) pieces of cotton calico to match top and bottom borders

For the trim: 1 2/3 yd (1.5m) of 3/4"- (2cm) wide rickrack

Pillow form: 14" x 14" (35.5cm x 35.5cm)

Rotary cutter

Self-healing cutting mat

Clear plastic ruler

FINISHED SIZE

To fit a 14" (35.5cm) square pillow form

SEAM ALLOWANCE

1/4" (6mm), unless otherwise noted

1. To create your photo patch, size your photo, keeping in mind that you will lose 1/4" (6mm) to the seam allowance on each side of the photo. Print the photo onto the sheet of printer-ready fabric in a "landscape" orientation, and cut out photo around the printed area (see Transferring Photos to Fabric [page 133]).

2. With right sides together and raw edges even, sew the top border strip to the top edge of the photo patch and the bottom border strip to the bottom edge of the photo patch. Press the seams toward the border strips. With right sides together and raw edges even, sew the side border strips to the photo patch piece. Press the seams toward the border strips.

3. For the pillow back, on one back piece turn under 1" (2.5cm) on the long edge and press; turn under 1" (2.5cm) again and press. Topstitch along each edge of the hem. Repeat for the other back piece.

4. Pin the rickrack trim around the outside edge of the front of the pillow, folding the rickrack over itself at a right angle at each corner. Baste, using a scant 1/4" (6mm) seam.

5. With the pillow front right side up, lay the 2 back pieces, right side down, on top of the pillow front; the back pieces will overlap (see photo). Pin all thicknesses together around the edges, and stitch.

6. Trim the corners. Turn right side out and press. Stuff with the pillow form.

TIP:

* Pillow covers generally start with a front piece that is cut to the exact size of the pillow form you intend to cover, or even a bit smaller for a nice, full look. If you will be covering a different size pillow than the one I used, be sure to adjust the size of your fabric pieces accordingly.

cupcake potholder

I love to cook with my eight-year-old niece. She's just old enough to handle certain grown-up tasks on her own (like measuring) and just young enough to still be intrigued by the difference between a measuring teaspoon and the teaspoon she uses for her cereal. As consummate cupcake connoisseurs, we frequently put our skills to good use in the sweet-treat department. We like to wield this special potholder when taking a dozen or two out of the oven.

MATERIALS

One kid's drawing, sized a bit smaller than 5" x 5" (12.5cm x 12.5cm) and at 200 dpi

For patch: One 8 1/2" x 11" (21.5cm x 28cm) sheet of ink-jet printer–ready fabric

For borders: Two 8" x 1 3/4" (20.5cm x 4.5cm) pieces and two 1 3/4" x 5 1/2" (4.5cm x 14cm) pieces of cotton print

For backing: One 10" x 10" (25.5cm x 25.5cm) piece of cotton print

For hanger: One 5" x 1 3/4" (12.5cm x 4.5cm) piece of cotton print (same fabric as backing)

For lining: Two 9" x 9" (23cm x 23cm) squares of cotton batting

Rotary cutter

Self-healing cutting mat

Clear plastic ruler

FINISHED SIZE

8" x 8" (20.5cm x 20.5cm)

SEAM ALLOWANCE

1/4" (6mm), unless otherwise noted

1. Scan and resize or color-copy your child's drawing to fit inside a finished 5" x 5" (12.5cm x 12.5cm) square. Print the image onto the ink-jet printer–ready fabric sheet (see Transferring Photos to Fabric [page 133]) and heat-set. With the drawing in the center, cut the fabric into a 5 1/2" x 5 1/2" (14cm x 14cm) square.

2. With right sides together, sew the short border strips to the side edges of the center square. Press the seams toward the border strips. Sew the long border strips to the top and the bottom of the center square piece. Press the seams toward the strips.

3. Place the potholder front right side up on the double layer of batting. Pin it in place, and baste around all 4 edges, using a scant 1/4" (6mm) seam. Trim away extra batting.

By Arden 8/1/07

4. To make the hanger loop, fold the hanger strip in half lengthwise and press. Open out and fold each long raw edge toward the center fold. Fold lengthwise on the center fold and press. Edge stitch down each long edge (the short edges will remain unfinished), and set hanger aside.

5. Place the backing fabric wrong side up on a flat surface. Center the potholder on the backing fabric square; you will have 1" (2.5cm) extra backing fabric on all sides. Pin the potholder in place and stitch in the ditch around the center patch (where the center patch meets the border strips) through all layers. Fold the backing fabric up over the edges of potholder, turning under 1/2" (13mm) and mitering the corners (see General Sewing Techniques [page 125]). Pin this border in place.

6. Fold the hanger piece in half. With the raw ends of the hanger together, slip the ends into the upper right-hand mitered corner of the binding, between the potholder top and the binding. Topstitch the binding in place around all 4 sides through all layers, running a few extra stitches along the mitered corner where the hanger protrudes to secure it. You're ready to bake!

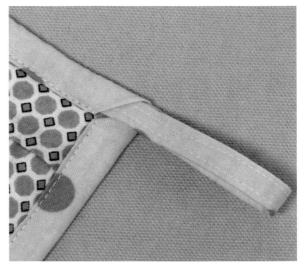

TIPS:

* Have your child draw a picture of something he or she likes to cook, using bright colors—markers and crayons work well and give you some color-saturated areas that will look good when printed onto fabric. Make sure your artist signs his or her work.

* Consider having your little cook embroider the fabric-printed drawing before cutting it from its 8½" x 11" (21.5cm x 28cm) sheet (but after you've removed the paper backing). Simple running stitches are easy for children to do and add an extra layer of interest to this utilitarian piece of art.

family recipe book

It's funny how you don't realize your family even has family recipes until you move away from home and start cooking for yourself. A craving for your mom's chicken 'n' dumplings—which was, of course, her mom's chicken 'n' dumplings—can strike most insistently when you least expect it. Not that your mom wouldn't love a recipe-requesting phone call, but now you can be prepared on those occasions when only comfort food will do. I designed this book cover around a photo album with 4" x 6" (10cm x 15cm) plastic sleeves, perfect for recipe cards. I asked my mother, my mother-in-law, and other relatives to contribute their specialties in their own handwriting— Thanksgiving stuffing, Grandma's spaghetti sauce, Swedish meatballs— and I add new recipes of my own all the time.

MATERIALS

Family Recipe Book templates (page 151)

Purchased photo album, any size

For the outside of the cover: One piece of heavyweight cotton the height of your album plus 1¼" (3cm) x the width of your album (front cover + back cover + spine) plus 1¼" (3cm)

For the flaps: Two pieces of heavyweight cotton the height of your album plus 1¼" (3cm) x 5" (12.5cm)

For the lining: One piece of cotton print, cut to the same size as the outside cover piece

For the corners: One 6"- (15cm-) diameter circle of Ultrasuede

For the ties: Two 10" (25.5cm) lengths of ½"- (13mm-) wide twill tape

Micron marker or fabric marker

Embroidery floss

Scalloped pinking shears

FINISHED SIZE

Can be made for any size album; pictured is 9" x 9" (23cm x 23cm) with a 2" (5cm) spine

SEAM ALLOWANCE

½" (13mm), unless otherwise noted

1. Using your computer, print out the text for your spine using a simple font at a size that will fit nicely both lengthwise and height-wise (I used Arial at 36-point size). Transfer the text and the embroidery designs from the Family Recipe Book templates to the outside piece of the book cover (see Embroidery [page 134]). With 2 strands of embroidery floss, embroider the text and the utensil elements, using back stitch and running stitch; use one strand of floss for the fine details.

2. To make the book cover corners, cut the Ultrasuede circle into equal pie-shaped quarters, and trim the curved edges with pinking shears. Baste the 4 pieces to the 4 outside cover corners. On the curves, sew with 3 strands of embroidery floss,

making running stitches on top of the basting stitches.

3. For a tie, fold under one end of one of the lengths of twill tape $1/4"$ (6mm) twice, and press flat. Using 3 strands of embroidery floss and running stitch, stitch along one long edge of the tie, around the folded end, and back along the other long edge, starting and stopping at the raw-edge end. Repeat for the other tie. Set ties aside.

4. For each cover flap, press in $1/4"$ (6mm) twice on one long edge and stitch close to the fold.

5. Center the ties on the short edges of the outside cover piece with the long ends of the ties lying loose toward the center of the piece, and baste. Lay the outside cover piece with right side facing up on a flat surface. With the raw edges even, place the flaps on either end of the outside cover piece, right side down. Place the lining, right side down, on top

of the stack (see photo). Pin the long edges of the stack and stitch down each long edge, using a $1/2"$ (13mm) seam.

6. Turn the cover inside out so that the outside cover piece is on one side, and the lining and the flaps are on the other. Press the long edges flat. Flip the flap around so that its right side faces the right side of the outside cover piece. Pin the short edge, keeping the tie flat with the long end toward the center, and stitch down the edge, using a scant $1/2"$ (13mm) seam. Repeat for the other end of the cover.

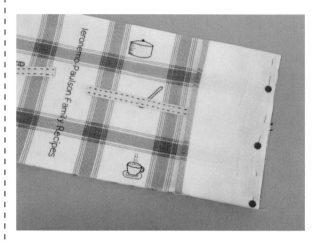

7. Trim the corners. Turn the book cover right side out, and press. Comfort food never had so much style!

TIPS:

* This is a tight-fitting cover, and should be measured, cut, and stitched carefully. In the last step, don't clip the corners until you're sure the cover fits your book.

* You can use a dishtowel for this project, or purchase dishtowel-like, decorator-weight fabric at most fabric stores. Simple plaids are popular and readily available.

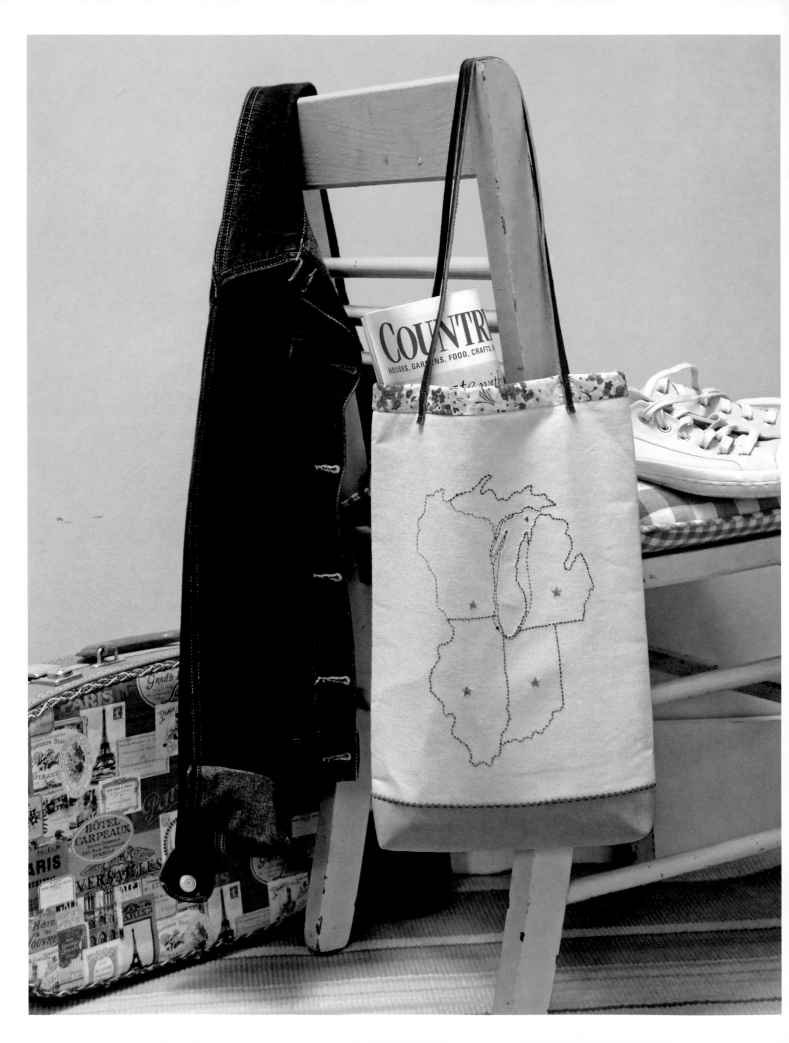

road-trip tote bag

When I was growing up in Chicago, every family vacation had Lake Michigan as its destination. For twenty years, we spent leisurely days at various cottages in Wisconsin and Michigan, always staying near the shore of that enchanted lake. The embroidery on this bag traces the outlines of our family's favorite summertime states and details our routes and destinations through the years.

The perfect size for a selection of magazines, a snack, and a map—the classic road-trip standbys—this tote could also be made before embarking on your journey, when you've set your itinerary but haven't yet had your adventure. If, at the end of your trip—beach-bronzed and blissed-out—you find yourself forgetting in which direction lies home, simply consult your embroidered map.

MATERIALS
For the bag: Two 11" x 16" (28cm x 40.5cm) pieces of heavyweight cotton canvas
For the interlining: Two 13" x 18" (33cm x 45.5cm) pieces of Timtex (roughly cut)
For the lining: Two 11" x 18" (28cm x 45.5cm) pieces of cotton print

For the bottom: Two 12" x 3" (30.5cm x 7.5cm) pieces of Ultrasuede
For the straps: Two 24" (61cm) lengths of 1/4" (6mm) leather lacing
Dressmaker's carbon paper
Micron marker or fabric marker
Embroidery floss
6" (15cm) embroidery hoop
Zigzag pinking shears

1/8" (3mm) hole punch
FINISHED SIZE
10 1/2" x 15 3/4 (27cm x 40cm) with 10 1/2" (26.5cm) straps
SEAM ALLOWANCE
1/4" (6mm), unless otherwise noted

1. To prepare your embroidery design, find a map of the area you'd like to transfer. Enlarge or reduce the elements of the map to a size that is about 2" (5cm) narrower than the width of the bag front piece and 8" (20.5cm) shorter than the length. Using dressmaker's carbon paper, transfer the outline of the regions of the map to the canvas bag front piece (see Embroidery [page 134]). Using a fabric marker or a fine-tip permanent marker, trace over the lines again to make the marks longer lasting. Draw the route of your trip by tracing another fine line, marking significant locations with a small dot.

2. Stitch all the elements of your trip design with 3 strands of embroidery floss in a running stitch. Use different colors for each state and very pale blue for the edges of any bodies of water. Stitch your route line in one strand of black floss in a running stitch, making French knots at the small dots. For the state capitals, make stars using 2 strands of gold floss in satin stitch. (See Embroidery [page 134].)

3. With pinking shears, trim one long edge of each Ultrasuede bottom piece. With right sides facing up, pin the front of the bag to the piece of Timtex. Pin the Ultrasuede piece along the bottom of bag, with the pinked edge toward the top. Baste the Ultrasuede piece across the front of the bag just below the pinked edge. Baste the front of the bag to the Timtex through all layers and around all edges.

4. Trim any extra Timtex and Ultrasuede so all edges are even with the bag front piece. Using 3 strands of embroidery floss in a running stitch, sew over the basting stitches below the pinked edge of the Ultrasuede piece. Repeat steps 3 and 4 to make the back of the bag.

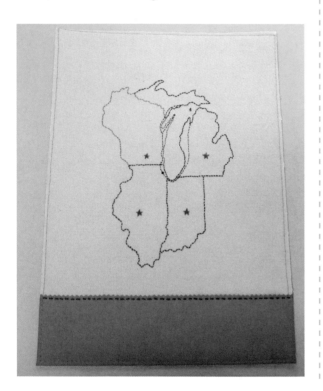

TIP:

* You can use any official map to create the embroidery design for this bag. If you need to transfer a design that is wider than it is long, you can easily adjust the dimensions of this bag to suit. Since it's based on a simple rectangle, you can make any size bag you need. Just cut your bag pieces to the dimensions you desire (adding ¼" [6mm] to all sides for the seam allowances) and make your linings 2" (5cm) taller than the bag pieces.

5. With the right sides of the bag pieces together, stitch the long edges and the bottom edge of bag. Stitch across the corners about 1" (2.5cm) from the edge to create 2 square bottom corners (see General Sewing Techniques [page 125]). Turn the bag right side out.

6. To make the lining, with the right sides of the 2 lining pieces together, stitch the long edges. Stitch across the bottom of the lining, leaving a 6" (15cm) opening through which you will turn the bag. Stitch across the corners about 1" (2.5cm) from the edge to create 2 square bottom corners (see General Sewing Techniques [page 125]).

7. With right sides together, place the outer bag into the lining (the outside of the lining will be facing you). With the top edges even, stitch around the top through all layers. Pull the outer bag through the opening in the lining. Turn in the edges of the lining opening and machine-sew the opening closed. Turn the lining to the inside, keeping 1" (2.5cm) of the lining showing on the outside of the top rim of the bag. Press the top edge of the bag, keeping the Timtex in the seam allowance flat and pressed toward the top.

8. For the straps, punch one hole in the leather lacing ¹/₄" (6mm) from the end of the lacing and another hole 1" (2.5cm) from the end. Repeat on each end of the two lengths of lacing. Mark the top edges of the bag 2" (5cm) from each side seam on the front and the back of the bag. Lay the end of one strap at one of the marks, 1 ¹/₄" (3cm) from the top of the bag. Using 3 strands of embroidery floss, stitch the strap to the bag through the holes. Repeat for the other 3 strap ends, being careful not to twist the lacing when attaching the opposite ends.

farmboy photo frame

This project was inspired by a photo of my husband carrying a bag of minidonuts and standing in a field of marigolds (who doesn't do this?) at a local farm, where the rows of flowers, fruits, and vegetables stretch toward the sunset. We were there in late summer, when the wealth of petals and produce is a feast for the eyes. I created this small quilted frame to mimic that colorful bounty. The strips of fabric that surround the center photo represent the furrowed rows in all their blooming glory. The guy in the picture is pretty cute, too.

MATERIALS

One photo, sized at 5 1/2" x 5 1/2" (14cm x 14cm) and 200 dpi

For photo patch: One 8 1/2" x 11" (21.5cm x 28cm) sheet of ink-jet printer–ready white fabric

For the frame: Forty-eight 1 1/2" x 4" (3.8cm x 10cm) pieces of assorted cotton prints

For the binding: 1 1/2" yd (1.6m) of 1" (2.5cm) double-fold binding

For the backing: One 14" x 14" (35.5cm x 35.5cm) piece of cotton print

For the lining: One 14" x 14" (35.5cm x 35cm) piece of Timtex

Rotary cutter

Self-healing cutting mat

Clear plastic ruler

Tape maker, 1" (2.5cm) size

Embroidery floss

FINISHED SIZE

12 1/2" x 12 1/2" (31.5cm x 31.5cm)

SEAM ALLOWANCE

1/4" (6mm), unless otherwise indicated

1. To make the photo patch, print the photo onto the ink-jet printer–ready fabric, following the directions in Transferring Photos to Fabric (page 133). There is a 1/2" (13mm) seam allowance built into this square, so center your subject accordingly. Cut out the photo around the printed area.

2. To make one side of the frame, with the right sides of 2 strips together, stitch them along the long edges. Join the other 11 strips in the same way. Press seams open. Repeat the process for the remaining 3 sides of the frame. Lay the 4 sides, right side up, in a square "frame" shape. Cut the end of each side at a 45-degree angle (pointing toward the center). Stitch the 4 pieces of the frame together at the angled ends, stopping 1/2" (13mm) short of the inner edge. Fold the inner edges of the 4 frame sides under and press.

3. Center the photo within the square of the frame, right side up. Pin the frame in place, and slip stitch the frame to the photo patch, keeping the photo taut and the edges of the seam allowances of the frame aligned with the edges of the photo patch (on the back side of the piece).

4. Lay the backing piece right side down. Lay the Timtex piece on top of the backing piece, and the frame piece, right side up, on top of the Timtex. The bottom layers are a bit larger than the frame piece so that it's easier to keep all layers lined up when stitching. Pin around all the edges of the piece, and baste through all layers 1/4" (6mm) from the edge. Stitch in the ditch around several of the strips to create a more textured look, if you wish. Trim the edges of the Timtex and the backing piece even with the frame piece.

5. Following directions in General Sewing Techniques (page 125), prepare and apply the binding around the edge of the frame.

6. To make the stitches by which the piece will hang, using 2 strands of embroidery floss, make a knotless start (see Hand-Sewing [page 130]) on the back of the piece in an upper corner, securing the thread to the Timtex and backing only (don't sew through to the front layer of the frame). Make a $1/2$" (13mm) stitch, running the needle back under the Timtex and backing only and coming up where you started. Repeat the $1/2$" (13mm) stitch and fasten off, burying the tails (see Hand-Sewing [page 130]) under the backing and snipping off the ends. Repeat for the opposite upper corner.

TIPS:

* Using a rotary cutter to cut the strips for the frame will greatly improve your chances of getting the edges straight.

* Let your photo and the memory it evokes guide your fabric selection. Choose prints that suit the season and the personality of the subject.

The nice thing about having a blog is that I find I look at things so differently. That's no metaphor—I mean it quite literally. I look at the back patio table, and I see it as a photo opportunity. I look at the ingredients for dinner, and I see a still life of pretty jars and baby leeks. I look at the pillows on the bed, and I see a collage of calicos I want to photograph.

The only reason I started taking photos of random stuff was because I got a digital camera that I *loved*. It was a Canon PowerShot A80. I loved the way it made everything look. It seemed like a magic box that could make even the most average scene sparkle and glow. I'd never been good at taking pictures before. I'd always figured it was something I just couldn't do. But Little Miss A80 was so good at making everything look pretty, whether or not her operator knew how to work the knobs and buttons. If you don't know much about photography, and you don't have much money to spend, and you don't already have a camera you love, I would just march down to the camera store and get this camera. Mine actually changed my life, and I mean that quite literally, too.

Because if you start taking photos of everyday life, you will start looking at everyday life differently. I think it just happens—you don't have to try. Through the viewfinder, I started looking around at my life and realized it looked pretty darn good, actually. Some days, in spite of the ubiquitous stacks of dirty dishes and piles of mail, it even looked beautiful. And I realized that not only did it *look* that way, it *was* that way. I had not noticed, not to such an extent, before it all started showing up, day after day, in my little camera. The evidence of how we've been blessed—with family, food, pets, a roof over our heads, warm blankets on our beds—is in a thousand photos I've taken over the past few

years. The pixels say it is so. Yours will, too. You need only pick up the camera and start pressing the shutter.

Nevertheless, as fabulous as most digital cameras are at helping us regular people take great pictures, there are a few things to know that will help make the photos you take reflect the world you see (and sometimes show you what you missed).

First, and most importantly, take *lots* of pictures. Lots and lots. Bring your camera with you everywhere, and brandish it liberally. Even the pros will tell you that some of the best shots come when you least expect them, after a hundred frames have already been taken and the session is thought to be over. You never know when that truly remarkable photo will allow itself to be captured, and the more you take, the better chance you have at getting it. The photo at right was one of dozens taken during our new puppy's first walk. It was a split second that captured that experience for her (skeptical but determined), and for us (encouraging but trying not to laugh) and it was a total surprise to see it there. Most of the photos we took of that walk came out blurry since she was moving around like crazy, but you just never know when you'll get one that's wonderful, and I'm so glad we have this now. Every time I look at it I start giggling. (She was walking like a pro not five minutes later, by the way, but that's why they call them "fleeting moments." You only get that one chance.)

Second, when taking photos of still lifes, the most important thing you can do to ensure a good-quality image is use a tripod. This sounds fancy, I know, but really, there is absolutely no substitute for it if you are trying to get that beautiful, crisp focus that makes your images sparkle. A tripod is inexpensive and easy to use once you get used to it. I'd be lost without mine, and drag it all

over the place when I want to get good shots in low light, or of things that don't move.

Third, learn a little about your photo editing software. You'll want to get comfortable with uploading and saving your photos, resizing them for viewing either on screen or on paper (or fabric), and cropping to enhance the composition. Tools like the "sharpening" filter and color balance settings can be simple to learn and experiment with—don't be intimidated by professional jargon or the incredible power of these programs. You really only need to do a couple of things to see a remarkable difference. Books and online tutorials, along with your camera's user manual, are rich with information and assistance. Some of my favorites are listed in the Resources section on page 143.

Lastly, throw all the technical stuff out the window and just have fun. It's not about getting the perfect shot. Pretend you *are* a photographer who knows what she's doing. Take pictures of everyone you can, whenever they'll let you. Point your camera at the flowers in your window boxes, the kids brushing their teeth, the puppies learning to heel, and all the cups and saucers you can find. Then see what surprises show up on film. Don't forget to point it at yourself, sometimes, too. Smile pretty, and say cheese. You're beautiful.

That one you knew.

felted-sweater bag

Let's say your favorite sweater were accidentally thrown in the laundry pile. Then let's say it accidentally landed in the washer and dryer. Then let's say your husband felt really bad about it. Then, of course, we'd have to say you couldn't get too mad because he was doing the laundry in the first place. But what to do with a once-beloved, now thick and tiny, felted sweater?

Make a handbag, of course! You don't have to have a laundry-room accident for this to be a great project, though. Any old, beloved wool pullover can be felted on purpose and stitched into a bag, allowing you to recycle well-worn sweaters into cool totes whenever you have a few you can't bear to part with.

MATERIALS

Two sweaters in complementary colors or patterns: One to felt and cut into two 13" x 11" (33cm x 28cm) pieces for bag front and back and one to felt and cut into one 9" x 6" (23cm x 15cm) piece for bag pocket

For lining: Two 13" x 11" (33cm x 28cm) pieces of cotton print

For lining pocket: Two 9" x 6" (23cm x 15cm) pieces of cotton print

For the straps: Two 24" (61cm) lengths of ¹/₄"- (6mm-) wide leather lacing

¹/₁₆" (1mm) hole punch

Pearl cotton #5

Dressmaker's chalk

Two vintage buttons

FINISHED SIZE

12 ¹/₂" x 10 ³/₄" (32cm x 27cm)

SEAM ALLOWANCE

¹/₄" (6mm), unless otherwise noted

1. To felt the sweaters, follow the instructions in General Sewing Techniques (page 125).

2. To trim the felted sweater into bag-sized pieces, lay it flat, with the ribbing toward the top (do not stretch the ribbing across the long edge). Cut straight across the sweater horizontally through both layers to make the bottom edges of the pieces, then measure and cut the sides. To make the bag front pocket piece, cut it from anywhere on the second sweater. Add curves to the bottom corners of the pocket by tracing the curve of a large button on the pocket piece and cutting smoothly along that line. Repeat this process to cut and shape the 2 lining pocket pieces.

3. To make the lining pocket, with right sides

together, stitch the 2 lining pocket pieces around the entire edge, leaving a 4" (10cm) opening in the bottom seam through which to turn the pocket. Clip the curves, turn the pocket right side out, and press, turning under the edges of the opening. Pin

the pocket in the center of the right side of one bag lining piece. Stitch around the sides and bottom of the pocket, leaving the top edge open and backstitching at each corner.

4. To make the lining, with right sides together, stitch down the side edges and across the bottom of the lining pieces. Stitch across the bottom corners about 1" (2.5cm) from the edge to create a square bottom (see General Sewing Techniques [page 125]). Leaving the lining wrong side out, turn under the top edge ¹/₂" (13mm), and press. Turn the lining right side out, and set it aside.

5. To make the bag front pocket, using the pearl cotton, blanket stitch across the top edge of the pocket and fasten off. Stitch the buttons to the

pocket (see photo) with regular thread. Pin the pocket to the center of the bag front piece, and baste. Attach the pocket to the bag front by blanket stitching with pearl cotton around the side and

TIP:

* Choose crew-neck or turtleneck sweaters that have high wool, angora, or mohair fiber content (at least 85 percent). Cardigans won't work, since you need to cut the sweater into two big pieces, and cottons, linens, and acrylics do not felt.

bottom edges of the pocket. (See Hand-Sewing [page 130].)

6. To make the bag, with right sides together, machine-sew down the side edges and across the bottom edge of the bag pieces. Stitch across the bottom corners about 1" (2.5 cm) from the edge to create a square bottom (see General Sewing Techniques [page 125]). Turn the bag right side out. Insert the lining into the bag with the wrong sides of the lining against the wrong sides of the bag, and then flip the bag so that the lining is on the outside. Pin the bag and lining together around the top, matching the side seams and keeping the folded edge of the lining 1/2" (13mm) below the top edge. Slip stitch the lining to the bag by hand using regular thread, slightly gathering the sweater ribbing as needed to fit. (See Hand-Sewing [page 130]). Flip the bag again so that the lining is now on the inside.

7. With dressmaker's chalk, mark the top edges of the bag 2" (5cm) from each side seam on the front and the back of the bag. For the straps, punch one hole in the leather lacing 1/4" (6mm) from the end of the lacing and another hole 1" (2.5cm) from the end. Repeat on each end of the two lengths of lacing. Lay the end of one strap at one of the marks, 1 1/4" (3cm) below the top of the bag. Using the pearl cotton, stitch the strap to the bag, through the holes. Repeat for the other 3 strap ends, being careful not to twist the lacing when attaching the opposite ends. (See Road-Trip Tote Bag photo [page 80] for guidance.)

brag book

This brag-book cover has an appliquéd photo of my dog, Audrey, the loveliest, most photographed, and most bragged about member of our little family. She passed away unexpectedly during the writing of this book, so this project, which was completed before she passed, has special significance for me. The simple sweetness of this design seems poignant and perfect for her, even more so now.

This little album is so versatile you could make one for anyone, or for any occasion. Consider creating one for each child or pet and adding your favorite photos of them over time. It would be perfect as a family album of photos sent by long-distance kids and grandkids, with the family name stamped across the twill tape. I also like the idea of creating an album just for Christmas, say, or just for one person's birthdays, so that themed photos could continue to be added chronologically every year.

MATERIALS

One photo, sized at 3" x 2" (7.5cm x 5cm) and 200 dpi

Purchased photo album, any size

For the outside of the cover: One piece of linen the height of your album plus $1^1/4$" (3cm) x the width of your album (front cover + back cover + spine) plus $1^1/4$" (3cm)

For the flaps: Two pieces of linen the height of your album plus 1" (2.5cm) x 5" (12.5cm)

For the lining: One piece cotton print, cut to the same size as the outside cover piece

For the trim: Enough $1/2$"- (13mm-) wide rickrack to go around all the edges of the cover, depending on how big your album is

For the photo patch: One $8^1/2$" x 11" (21.5cm x 28cm) piece of cotton muslin

For the nametag: 18" (45.5cm) $1/2$"- (13mm-) wide twill tape

For the ties: Two 10" (25.5cm) lengths of $1/2$"- (13mm-) wide ribbon

One $8^1/2$" x 11" (21.5cm x 28cm) piece of full-sheet sticker paper

Rotary cutter

Self-healing cutting mat

Clear plastic ruler

Alphabet rubber stamps

Permanent-ink stamp pad in a contrasting color

Embroidery floss in the same contrasting color

4" (10cm) embroidery hoop

Bubble-jet setter

SEAM ALLOWANCE

$1/2$" (13mm), unless otherwise noted

1. To create your photo patch, treat the muslin piece and the twill tape (though you'll use that later) with the bubble-jet setter (see Transferring Photos to Fabric [page 133]). When the muslin is dry, smooth the sticker paper to the wrong side of the fabric. On your computer, size your photo to about 3" (7.5cm) wide x 2" (5cm) high, and print it onto the center of your muslin piece. Peel off the sticker paper and heat-set the ink with a warm iron.

Using 3 strands of embroidery floss, embroider the edges of the image with running stitches (see Hand-Sewing [page 130].) Trim the photo leaving a 1" (2.5cm) border of muslin around the edge.

2. Press under $1/2$" (13mm) on all edges of your photo patch. To find the center of the front of the book cover, first find the center of the front of your album: Measure the width of your album

and divide that by 2; measure the height of your album and divide that measurement by 2. Add $^1/_2$" (13mm) to each of these 2 measurements. The center point of the front of the cover lies at the intersection of these height and width axes as measured from the bottom right corner of the cover front piece. Using a clear ruler to help you, center your photo over the center point and slip stitch it to the cover by hand (see Hand-Sewing [page 130]).

3. To make the name tag, stamp letters onto the twill tape, using the alphabet stamps and permanent ink. (First practice on extra twill tape until you get a good rendering.) Cut and tack

the name tag under the photo with 3 strands of embroidery floss.

4. For each cover flap, press in $^1/_4$" (6mm) on one long edge twice and stitch close to the fold. Set the flaps aside.

5. Pin the rickrack trim around the outside edge of the outside cover piece, folding the rickrack downward (making a right angle) at each corner and keeping the center of the trim on the seam line, $^1/_2$" (13mm) from the edge. Baste the rickrack to the cover using a $^1/_4$" (6mm) seam.

6. For the ties, lay the outside cover piece facing up on a flat surface. Center the ribbon with the long ends lying loose toward the center of the cover

and baste. With the raw edges even place the flaps on either end of cover, right side down. Place the lining, right side down, on top of the stack (see photo). Pin the 2 long edges of the stack and stitch down each edge using a $^1/_2$" (13mm) seam.

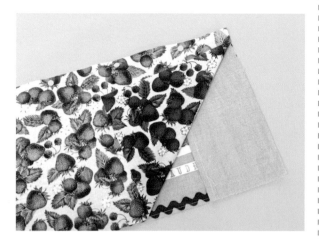

7. Turn the cover inside out so that the outside piece is on one side and the lining and the flaps are on the other. Press the long edges flat. Flip the flap around so that its right side faces the right side of the outside cover piece. Pin the short edges of the outside piece, flap, and lining, catching the ribbon, and stitch down the edge, using a $^1/_2$" (13mm) seam. Repeat for the other end of cover.

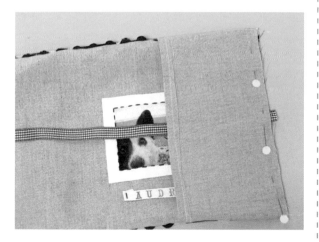

8. Trim the corners. Turn the book cover right side out, and press.

TIP:

* I wanted a rustic look for this image, so I treated some muslin before printing on it. The weave of the muslin is not as fine as the weave of some of the more expensive pretreated ink-jet printer–ready fabric sheets, but to me the cover linen, the strawberry print lining, and the gingham ribbon called for an image that was faded and homey. If you prefer an image that reads more crisply, just use ink-jet printer–ready fabric for the photo patch.

From all my waxing profoundly about Sweatpants Tuesdays, you might think I don't have a closet full of glad rags. But I do. Special occasions roll around just often enough for me to get very dressed up, and very excited. I love special events because they often bring everyone together, in our nicest clothes, at a fancy location, and on our best behavior (or, at least, with our best intentions). Getting people together in one place and time can be nothing short of a miracle these days; with families living far apart and schedules overloaded, time together feels precious and, often, far too rare. As I get older, I realize what my older relatives have known all along—that special occasions are distinct and completely unrepeatable moments.

Because special occasions are special by virtue of their not being everyday events, they tend to create a certain amount of stress, especially for the organizers. As much as we want to relax, enjoy, and celebrate the event and each other, there are inevitable details that must be attended to. While running (or recovering from) the marathon of preparations that weddings, holidays, and other big parties require, it can be a blessing just to sit for a few hours, nothing in your hand but a needle. Here, on the sofa or in the sewing room, the Mobius strip of your mind can untwist, straighten, and smooth itself as the stitches add up.

Before I was even engaged to be married, I knew I would sew my own wedding dress. When the time came, I was a student and he was a dishwasher/geologist and we lived, then, in the mountains of western Montana. Far from my sewing-inclined friends, I had to pin and fit the bodice on myself in the mirror. I made the dress in our tiny studio apartment, my sewing machine on the breakfast table (the only table), my cat next to me on the sofa watching as I wearily contemplated the seven yards of ¼" ribbon that needed to be hand-stitched to the billowing organza hem of the skirt. I thought that would be the worst part, coming at the very end as it did, when I was so tired and ready to be done not only with the dress but with the whole wedding.

How could I have known that attaching that shimmering strip of ribbon would turn out to be one of the best parts? The wedding day itself months later was, as so many people had warned, kind of a blur. But those quiet Sunday afternoons I spent stitching the hem of the enormous white pouf of my dress, yard after yard of silk ribbon spilling to the floor by my side, the sun setting in a haze of pink, have stayed with me. Because as I stitched I thought about Andy: Andy laughing in the truck as we drove through the mountains, Andy bringing a collection of enormous (and, to my eye, very plain-looking) rocks with him when he came to live with me in Montana, Andy rolling out a new blue bicycle as a gift for me, Andy looking bewildered immediately after our first kiss years before and saying, simply, "Wow."

When I look at the dress now, those things are what I see. When I'm sewing for special occasions—birthdays, holidays, weddings, and other remarkable days—it's impossible for me not to slow down, remember people, and think about how things have changed—and how much has stayed the same.

- - - - - - -

Of course, special-occasion sewing is not limited to stitching your own enormous handmade wedding dress. There are much easier ways to commemorate weddings, or any special occasion. Sewing for special days needn't be daunting or difficult. Don't think you must only attempt perfectly executed heirlooms. The requirements for these projects range from simple cutting and hand-sewing, as on the Wedding Rehearsal Corsage, to the straightforward but time-consuming, like the Nutcracker Doll and the Wedding Guestbook Wall Hanging. Most of them require more patience than skill, so I hope you will allow yourself a few quiet hours to sit still, stitch, and reflect on everyone and everything that has led up to the special day you're sewing for.

▶ *My wedding dress: yards of organza gathered over a silk skirt, trimmed with ribbon and lots of love.*

This festive banner is so sweet, and you can hang it up every year on that special day. If you use new fabrics for the banner, it will be fun to see how the fabrics become dated over the years, marking the place in time when you chose them. The project will take you a while to complete, but it's a keeper. Take a picture of its recipient smiling under it every year, as the candles add up.

MATERIALS

Birthday Banner template (page 152)

For scallops: Fifteen pairs (for HAPPY BIRTHDAY and spaces) plus one pair for each letter of the person's name 6" x 6" (15cm x 15cm) pieces cut from assorted cotton prints

For hanger: About 3 yd (2.75m) of 1" (2.5cm) purchased double-fold binding, depending on length of person's name

Masking tape

Dressmaker's chalk

Freezer paper

Small scissors, or X-acto knife and self-healing cutting mat

Fabric paint

Small paintbrush

Scalloped or zigzag pinking shears

FINISHED SIZE

105" (267cm) for banner shown

1. Arrange your fabric pieces in a pleasing order. Each scalloped piece will need 2 pieces—one for the front and one for the back. On small pieces of masking tape, write each letter, including spaces, that you will need to spell out your message. Stick each letter or space to the top piece of each pair of fabrics to identify which letter goes on which piece. Set the pieces aside.

2. To make the stencils, use your computer to print out your message—HAPPY BIRTHDAY [NAME]—in a font that is easy to read and to cut out, sized to about 1 1/2" (3.8cm) high (I used Georgia at 250-point size). Following the instructions in Freezer-Paper Stenciling (page 139), prepare a stencil for each letter.

3. Using dressmaker's chalk (not a fabric marker, since you will be ironing these scallops before you cut them out, and you don't want to risk making the ink permanent by heat-setting it), trace the Scallop template onto the top piece of each pair of fabrics. Following instructions in Freezer-Paper Stenciling (page 139), iron each letter stencil to its scallop, centering it horizontally and toward the bottom of each scallop. Then paint. Use 2 coats of paint if you need to.

4. When the paint is dry, peel each stencil off the scallop and heat-set the fabric paint. Then place the scallop piece on another square of the same fabric, wrong sides together. Machine-sew around the entire scallop on the chalk outline. Cut around the curved part of each scallop, using pinking shears and trimming close to the stitch line. Use regular scissors to trim 1/8" (3mm) above the stitching across the top of the scallop. Repeat for each scallop, including the ones containing spaces (which you've left blank).

5. Press the center fold of the binding open down the entire length of the tape. Lay the tape out on the floor, right side down. Leaving an 18" (45.5cm) length of the tape at the front end (this will turn into a loop for hanging), lay the scallops, right sides up and with the tops even with the center fold

line, along the length of the tape, spelling out the message. To make the banner shorter, overlap the scallops; to make it longer, spread them out (adjust the length of the ends left to use as hanging loops accordingly). Cut the tape, leaving an 18" (45.5cm) length at the end.

6. Fold the cut ends of the tape in $1/2$" (13mm) to finish them, then fold the entire length of the tape down over the tops of the scallops. Pin the tape along the entire banner, securing all layers of tape and scallop pieces. Stitch down the short edge of the tape, then down the entire length, and up the short edge at the opposite end of banner. Fold over 6" (15cm) on each end, and tack with a few stitches to make a 3" (7.5cm) loop at each end for hanging.

TIPS:

* Choose color-coordinated fabrics with simple patterns that won't compete with the stenciled letters. Also consider the color of paint you want to use for your letters when choosing the fabrics. All the letters should be readable from a distance.

* You may be able to use stencils for repeated letters two and even three times. Make sure the paint on the stencil is completely dry before you iron the stencil on again, so you don't get paint on the bottom of your iron.

* If the birthday celebrant's name is long, consider splitting the banner into two parts—one for HAPPY BIRTHDAY and one for the person's name. It will be easier to hang a banner if it's not super-duper long.

peppermint-heart garland

My husband's family is Swedish, and I love the tradition of red-and-white heart decorations in Swedish culture, especially popular at Christmastime. This pretty, personalized garland, made of soft stenciled-and-embroidered hearts, looks darling hung across a child's headboard every holiday season, like a dream of peppermint. You could even leave it up all year 'round, and through December hang tiny, purchased socks from small clips between the hearts to fill with bedtime treats—little dolls or animals, tiny books, or love notes wishing your little one sweet dreams.

MATERIALS

Peppermint-Heart Garland template (page 153)

For hearts: Nine pairs of 6" x 6" (15cm x 15cm) pieces of cotton fabric in assorted calicos, solids, and stripes

For heart hangers: Nine 8" (20.5cm) lengths of ¹/₂"- (13mm-) wide twill tape

For garland: 1 ¹/₂ yd (1.4m) of ³/₄"- (17mm-) wide ribbon, or length needed to string between bedposts

Freezer paper

Small scissors, or X-acto knife and self-healing cutting mat

Fabric paint

Small paintbrush

Embroidery floss

Polyester or wool fiberfill

FINISHED SIZE

51" (130cm), for garland shown

SEAM ALLOWANCE

¹/₄" (6 mm), unless otherwise noted

1. Trace the Heart template onto one wrong side of each pair of fabric pieces and cut out all 18 heart pieces.

2. To make the stencils, use your computer to print out the letters of your child's name in a font that is easy to read and to cut out, sized to about 1 ¹/₂" (3.8cm) high (I used Send Flowers, at 400-point

size). Following the instructions in Freezer-Paper Stenciling (page 139), prepare a stencil for each letter. Stencil each letter onto the right side of the right side of the front fabric piece of each heart pair and heat set.

3. To make the heart hangers, lay two heart pieces together, right sides facing. Fold one twill tape hanger in half, and lay it between the front and

TIP:

* Directions are given here for 5 letter hearts and 4 plain hearts strung into a 45" (114cm) garland. If your child's name has more or fewer letters, adjust fabric amounts and garland length accordingly.

back pieces of the heart with the loop hanging down toward the heart point and the raw edges even with the top of the heart pieces. Pin around the heart, and stitch (catching the raw edges of the hanger in the seam), leaving a 1 1/2" (3.8cm) opening on one side of the heart. Clip the seam curves and point (see General Sewing Techniques [page 125]). Turn the heart right side out, and press.

4. Stuff the heart lightly with fiberfill or wool batting. Whipstitch the opening closed. Using 3 strands of embroidery floss and a running stitch, outline the heart 1/8" (3mm) from the edge. Hide the tails of the floss in the body of the heart. (See Hand-Sewing [page 130].)

5. Repeat steps 3 and 4 for the remaining hearts.

6. To string the hearts on the ribbon, run the ribbon through the hangers, placing the center letter of the child's name halfway along the length of the ribbon. Space the hearts evenly and pin each one in place. Using 3 strands of embroidery floss, tack each hanger to the ribbon with an embroidered X. To make a 2" (5cm) loop at each end of the ribbon for hanging, fold under the ends of the ribbon 1/2" (13mm), then fold over 4" (10cm) on each end, and tack with a few stitches.

nutcracker doll

We got dressed up and took our niece to see The Nutcracker *last winter. It was her first time at the ballet in the big auditorium downtown and, sitting next to her in the dark, watching snowflakes and sugarplums and sparkly tutus, I fell in love with Clara, the main character, all over again. To commemorate that winter afternoon, I made my niece a Clara-inspired doll and presented it to her at Christmas. This basic doll is so easy to adapt—change gender, hair color, eye color, skin color, and clothing to look like a special character, relative, or friend in your child's life.*

MATERIALS

Nutcracker Doll template (page 154)

For head: Two 6" x 6" (15cm x 15cm) pieces of skin-colored cotton

For legs: Two 3 1/4" x 11" (8.5cm x 28cm) pieces of skin-colored cotton

For bodice: Two 3 3/4" x 5 3/8" (9.5cm x 13.5cm) pieces of cotton print

For sleeves: Two 2 3/8" x 6 1/2" (6cm x 16.5cm) pieces of cotton print in the same fabric as the bodice

For hands: Two 2 3/8" x 1" (6cm x 2.5cm) pieces of skin-colored cotton

For hair: 15 yd (14m) of worsted-weight wool yarn

For hair bows: 1/3 yd (30.5cm) of 7mm-wide silk embroidery ribbon (ribbon A)

For skirt: One 12" x 20" (30.5cm x 51cm) piece of cotton print

For skirt trim: 2/3 yd (61cm) of eyelet trim (to go around bottom of skirt)

For skirt belt: 2/3 yd (61cm) of 4mm-wide silk embroidery ribbon (ribbon B)

Embroidery floss in several different colors for eyes, nose, and mouth

4" (10cm) embroidery hoop

Red ink stamp pad

Small paintbrush

Polyester fiberfill or wool batting

Toy-stuffing tool or hemostat

Heavyweight thread to match skin color

Big sharp needle (yarn darner)

Small pieces of colored felt, or purchased paper or sequin flower

Fabric glue

FINISHED SIZE

18" (45.5cm) tall

SEAM ALLOWANCE

1/4" (6mm), unless otherwise noted

1. To embroider the doll's face, trace the front of the doll's head (using the Head template) onto the right side of one piece of the head fabric. Transfer the face markings to the fabric using one of the transfer methods discussed in Embroidery (page 134). Cut out the face, leaving several inches (about 8cm) of fabric around the traced lines so that you can center the face in the embroidery hoop. Embroider the facial features using 2 strands of embroidery floss: Satin stitch the eyes and lips, and backstitch the nose. With a small paintbrush, dab a bit of red ink from the stamp pad onto the cheeks.

When you're finished making the face, remove the embroidery hoop and cut out the front of the head along the traced lines. Trace the head onto the other fabric piece and cut out for the back.

2. With the right sides together, machine-sew the hand pieces to the ends of the sleeve pieces, and the head pieces to the tops of the bodice pieces. Fold the sleeve/hand piece lengthwise with right sides together and stitch the long edge, leaving the top of the sleeve and the bottom of the hand open for stuffing. Repeat for the second arm. Put the right sides of the head/bodice pieces together and stitch around the edges of the sides and head, leaving the bottom open for stuffing. Fold the leg piece lengthwise with right sides together and stitch the long edge, leaving the top of the leg and the bottom of the foot open for stuffing. Repeat for the second leg.

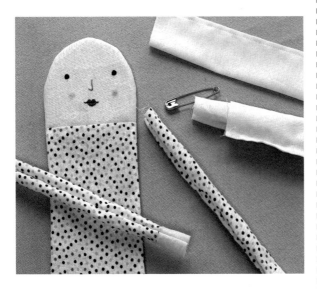

3. Trim the seams slightly and clip all curves. Turn the pieces right side out, and stuff them (see Tip on next page). Turn under the edges of the top arm and leg openings and hand-stitch the openings closed. Sew a line of running stitches around the bottom edge of the hands and feet, and pull gathers tight to close, tucking the seam allowance in and securing with a knot to finish. Bury the end of the thread in the limb of the doll, for each

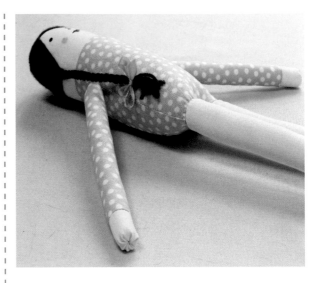

limb. Whipstitch each arm securely to the body with a heavyweight thread. Insert the top of the leg into the bodice, folding in the edges of the bodice around the leg and whipstitching to secure. Repeat for the other leg.

4. To make the hair, thread a big, sharp needle (a yarn darner, size 14 or 16, works well [see Resources, page 143]) with an 18" (45.5cm) strand of yarn. On one side of the head, stitch the hair from her "part" (at the top of the head) to her ear (on the seam), across the forehead. Following the hairline, continue stitching across the front and top of the head. Repeat for the other side of the hair, and then repeat for both sides of the back, going in with the needle along a "part" back down the center. When your yarn is getting short, hide the end within the head to finish: Just clip the yarn close to the fabric and push it in. To make the braids, thread the needle with a 12" (30.5cm) strand of yarn. Sew the strand under and back out at the ear, so each half of the length of the yarn hangs on each side of the "ear." Repeat twice; you will have 6 strands, 3 on each side. With 3 clumps of 2 strands each, braid the hair, fastening the end tightly with a bow of ribbon A.

5. To make the skirt, sew the short sides of the skirt piece together, right sides facing each other,

forming a loop. Press under a hem on each long edge of the loop. Fold the loop in half lengthwise with wrong sides together and press the fold. Insert the raw edge of the trim between the folded edges of the skirt hem; pin and machine-sew around. Using heavyweight thread, run a row of long basting stitches by hand around the waistline of the skirt (the folded edge) about $1/4$" (6mm) below the fold, starting and ending at the seam of the loop (the seam will be the back of the skirt). Place the skirt on the doll and pull up the gathers to fit. Use the tails of the gathering thread to tack the skirt to the bodice with a few stitches. Bury the thread in the bodice of the doll, and trim the ends. Tie ribbon B around her waist, making a bow in the front.

6. Cut small flowers out of felt and tack them with small stitches to the doll's head for decoration if the doll will be played with a lot, or glue a purchased paper or sequined flower if she's more the "sit and look pretty" type.

TIPS:

* Stuffing the skinny legs and arms of this doll can be frustrating. I highly recommend purchasing a toy-stuffing fork or a hemostat (see Resources [page 143]).

* Sewing the yarn doll hair through the doll's head can be tough on your fingers. Consider using a thimble or a rubber finger protector. Twist the needle back and forth as you bring it through the fabric.

monogrammed stocking

Christmas stockings are one of those things that bring back memories every time you pull them out of the box. Even though you can't pack as much into them, I prefer the ones that look like they just slipped off someone's foot—you really have to dig deep to pull out the smallest treasures stuffed into the toe. These monogrammed beauties combine rustic wools with homey details like buttons, blanket stitches, and calicos for a hodgepodge of Dickensian charm, perfect for a traditional or whimsical Christmas mantel, and sure to be used year after year.

MATERIALS

Monogrammed Stocking template (page 155)

For the stocking: 5/8 yd (57cm) of plaid woven wool, any width

For the stabilizer: 2/3 yd (61cm) of lightweight fusible stabilizer

For the lining: 1/3 yd (30.5cm) of 45"- (114cm-) wide cotton print

For the monogram patch: One 4" x 6" (10cm x 15cm) piece of wool felt

Small (about 1/2" [13mm]), flat buttons in assorted colors

For the toe and heel patches: Two 6" x 6" (15cm x 15cm) pieces of cotton print

For the top binding and hanger: 2/3 yd (61cm) 1" (2.5cm) double-fold binding

Tape-maker, 1" (2.5cm) size

Embroidery floss to contrast with felt color

Dressmaker's carbon paper

FINISHED SIZE

About 18" (45.5cm) long x 12" (30.5) wide

SEAM ALLOWANCE

1/4" (6mm), unless otherwise noted

1. Enlarge the Stocking template to the percentage specified. Place the template right side up on the wool fabric, aligning grain as desired. Trace and cut 2 stocking pieces, 2 stabilizer pieces, and 2 lining pieces (lining fabric does not have to be cut on the bias). Following the manufacturer's instructions, iron the stabilizer pieces onto the wrong sides of the stocking pieces. Set aside.

2. To make the monogram patch, use your computer to print out a simple letter sized to about 4" (10cm) tall (I used Andale Mono at 430-point size). Trace the letter onto the felt patch using dressmaker's carbon paper (see Embroidery [page 134]). Stitch small buttons along the outline of the letter. Place the patch on the front of the stocking about 2" (5cm) below the top. Blanket stitch the patch to the stocking front, using 3 strands of embroidery floss (see Hand-Sewing [page 130]).

3. To make the toe and heel patches, cut 2 toe pieces and 2 heel pieces and baste each patch to the stocking around all edges. Decorate the inside curves of the patches using 3 strands of embroidery floss and a blanket stitch. Place the front and back stocking pieces right sides together, and stitch around the stocking, leaving the top open and catching the toe and heel patches smoothly in the seam. Clip the curves, and turn the stocking right side out. Remove basting stitches on the toe and heel patches.

4. To make the lining, put the right sides of the 2 lining pieces together and stitch around the

stocking lining, leaving the top open. Trim the seam to ¹/8" (3mm). Leaving the wrong side out, insert the lining into the stocking, matching the top edges evenly. Baste around the top.

5. To make the binding, see General Sewing Techniques (page 125). To make the stocking hanger (loop), cut a 7" (18cm) length of the tape and fold in half lengthwise. Edge stitch down each long edge, and set the hanger aside. Attach the binding to the top of the stocking (see General Sewing Techniques [page 125]), folding the hanger in half and slipping the ends under the binding at the side seam before machine-sewing.

TIPS:

★ Plaid woolens look interesting when cut on the bias, so I've allowed for that extra fabric in the materials list. If you're using tweed or a solid-colored wool, you'll only need ¹/3 yd (30.5cm).

★ I like to lay out all the buttons I'll be using on the printed paper copy of the monogram. I play with the arrangement to get the buttons nicely spaced and the colors evenly balanced. To sew the buttons to the felt patch, pick them up one at a time and stitch.

I have a weakness for vintage sewing notions and fabric the way other girls love chocolate. I'll take a box of old buttons over a dozen truffles any day.

If you are lucky enough to have inherited a stash of fabric, a bag of trims, or a sewing box of ribbons from someone who learned to sew long ago, consider yourself the envy of the rest of us. If you're one of those sewers who gnash their teeth when they see pretty vintage treasures in books and magazines but have no idea where one would find such supplies, you're in luck. Because here's the weird thing: In my experience, when it comes to these one-of-a-kind seemingly hard-to-find bits and baubles, you need only ask in order to receive.

For years, I had only the smallest, most precious-to-me little collection of vintage velvet strawberries, plastic buttons from the '60s, and robin's-egg-blue rickrack. I hoarded it compulsively. I haunted antique stores for notions, and was appalled at how expensive they were to buy. My collection remained small and precious, and I was loath to use it up, lest I never find more, lest there was no more in the world.

But then one day I mentioned to somebody that I really loved old sewing things, and the next thing I knew I was getting a box of them from that person's neighbor-down-the-street's mother, who was having a garage sale and selling the box not five minutes after I mentioned my

special need to my friend. See how that works? The more people I told I was looking for these things, the more I discovered that not everyone loves these things, and some people are actually *getting rid* of these things. And then they'd give them to me. It's true. All over the world, boxes of sewing notions wait in garages for you. You need only ask the universe, or start mentioning how much you love them to any and all acquaintances and passersby for vintage sewing supplies to start falling into your lap.

If you feel you really can't wait for millinery flowers and calico bias trim to find you, you can also check my Resources on page 143 for some great sources. They won't be free, mind you. But I would never fault you for splurging. I would totally and completely understand.

Mollie and Evan · August 2, 2008

Wouldn't this corsage be lovely for a bride to wear to her shower or rehearsal dinner? The frothy blossom is so easy to make that you might consider creating an entire bouquet of them. Cotton lawn is the perfect fabric for this corsage, since it is finely woven, soft, and lightweight. When the petals are gathered around the stamen, they have a peony-like quality. And you can print any message (like the happy couple's names and the wedding date) on the "leaves." Turn this corsage into a Mother's Day gift by printing children's names instead of a wedding date, or, since they're so fast to whip up and personalize, make them to give as favors at a bridal or baby shower.

MATERIALS

Wedding Rehearsal Corsage templates (page 156)

For flower layers: Two 12" x 9" (30.5cm x 23cm) pieces of cotton lawn in complementary colors

For stamen: Three vintage millinery stamens (or one plastic berry on a 1 1/2" [3.8cm] wire stem, snipped from a spray of plastic berries)

For flower back: One 2" (5cm) circle of wool felt

For leaves: One 9" (23cm) length of rayon seam trimming

Zigzag pinking shears

Upholstery thread in a color to match petals

1/8" (3mm) hole punch

1" (2.5cm) bar pin (available at craft stores)

Fabric glue

Hot glue gun

Dressmaker's chalk

Double-sided tape

Scotch tape

FINISHED SIZE

5" (12.5cm) in diameter

SEAM ALLOWANCE

1/4" (6mm)

1. To make the bottom layer of flower petals, fold one sheet of the fabric in half lengthwise and crosswise until you have a folded piece that is 16 layers thick. Using regular scissors, slice through all the folds of the stack so that the layers of fabric are separate and lying flat. With dressmaker's chalk, trace the Large Petal template onto the top layer of the stack. Cut out the stack of 16 petals with pinking shears, just inside the traced line. Repeat with the other sheet of fabric for the top layer of smaller petals, using the Small Petal template.

2. Thread a needle with an 18" (46cm) length of upholstery thread. String the bottom layer of petals (the large petals) right side up using loose running stitches, 1/4" (6mm) from the bottom edge of the petal. Bunch the petals toward the middle of the length of thread and tie the thread in a square knot, leaving the tails of thread hanging under the petal layer. Repeat for the top layer (the small petals).

3. Thread the 2 tails of the top layer back onto the needle. Lay the top layer of petals on top of the bottom layer, right side up, and push the threaded needle through the bottom edge of a petal on the bottom layer of petals. All 4 tails should now be hanging under the flower. Tie the tails together in a tight square knot, and trim the ends to about 1/2" (13mm).

4. Push the wire ends of the stamens through all layers of the flower through the hole in the center of the stacked rings of petals. Under the flower, bend the wires at a 45-degree angle. Fuss with the petals a bit to ease the gathers evenly around both layers of the flower. Put a dab of glue over the thread tails and the wire stem of the stamen to hold them in place.

5. Using the hole punch, punch 2 holes 1" (2.5cm) apart, centered, through the circle of wool felt. Open the bar pin and push the sharp end up through one hole and the closing mechanism up through the other hole. Close the pin. Using fabric glue, glue the circle of felt and pin back to the back of the flower, covering the thread tails and the wire. Use the hot glue gun to push some glue between the top and bottom petal layers near the center of the flower, to secure the stamen wire and give the flower more stability.

6. To make the leaves, using your computer, create a document with a "landscape" orientation (so your type will run horizontally across the wide measurement of a letter-size piece of paper). Use a readable font in a size slightly smaller than the width of the rayon trimming (I used Send Flowers at 28-point size). Leave about 1 1/2" (3.8cm) between the name and the date so that you can tie the rayon trimming around the stamen without squishing the text. Using a piece of double-sided tape, secure a strip of rayon trimming directly on top of the names you've printed on the paper, making sure the trimming is lying smooth at both ends. (You can use a piece of Scotch tape to secure the end of the trimming that will go through the printer first.) Run the paper through the printer again, and voilà—printed trimming. Tie the piece evenly around the stamen of the flower. Trim the ends into sharp points like leaves.

TIP:

* If you don't have your own collection of vintage millinery supplies, Tinsel Trading in New York is a wonderland of bits and baubles. You can order from the company's vast inventory online (see Resources [page 143]). You will also find stems of artificial berries at craft and fabric stores that sell silk flowers: They come in all sorts of finishes, from glittery to smooth plastic coated. Just use a wire snipper to cut berries from their stems, leaving a 1½" (3.8cm) length of wire, which you will poke through the center of the flower to hold all the petal layers together.

wedding-shoe bag

Wedding attire is special stuff. Even though you know full well you'll only wear those shoes once, it's still hard to keep yourself from getting exactly the pair you want. This little Tiffany-blue bag can be used to keep them tucked away for posterity. Embroidered with a vintage flower garland and monogram, the bag can also be used for lingerie, or even wedding cards or other special keepsakes. Its simple eyelet trims add a sweet touch.

MATERIALS

Wedding-Shoe Bag template (page 157)

For the bag and lining: Four 11 1/2" x 14 1/2" (29cm x 37cm) pieces of solid-color cotton

For the top trim: One 23" (58.5cm) piece of 3/4"- (2cm-) wide eyelet trim, finished on one edge

For the bag trim: Two 12" (30.5cm) pieces of 1"- (2.5cm-) wide eyelet trim, finished on both edges

For the ties: Two 18" (45.5cm) lengths of 1/2"- (13mm-) wide ribbon

White embroidery floss

Micron marker or fabric marker

6" (15cm) embroidery hoop

FINISHED SIZE

11" x 14" (28cm x 35.5cm)

SEAM ALLOWANCE

1/4" (6mm), unless otherwise noted

1. Enlarge the Wreath template (page 157) to the percentage specified. Print a monogram (I used a font called Café Aroma in a 200-point size). Cut around the monogram, center the initial in the wreath, and tape it in place. Transfer the design to the bag front piece and embroider with 2 strands of embroidery floss, using back stitch and satin stitch

(see Hand-Sewing [page 130] and Embroidery [page 134]). Press.

2. Pin the double-edged eyelet trim to the bag front, with the bottom edge of the trim 2 1/2" (6.5cm) from the bottom edge of the bag front. Machine-sew each long edge of the trim. Repeat for the bag back.

3. With the right sides of the bag together, on each side seamline mark a 1" (2.5cm) opening 1 1/4" (3cm) from the top of the bag. Stitch the 2 side seams and the bottom seam of the bag, backstitching on both sides of the 2 openings. Stitch across the corners about 1" (2.5cm) from the edge to create 2 square bottom corners (see General Sewing Techniques [page 125]). Turn the bag right side out.

4. To make the lining, with the right sides of the 2 lining pieces together, stitch the long edges. Stitch

across the bottom of the lining, leaving a 4" (10cm) opening in the bottom seam through which to turn the bag. Stitch across the corners about 1" (2.5cm) from the edge to create 2 square bottom corners (see General Sewing Techniques [page 125]).

5. To make the top trim, stitch the ends of the trim together with a French seam: With the **wrong** sides together, stitch the short ends of the trim together using a 1/4" (6mm) seam, creating a loop. Trim the seam to 1/8" (3mm). Turn the loop wrong side out. With the right sides together, at the first seam stitch a second seam 1/4" (6mm) from the edge, enclosing the first seam allowance.

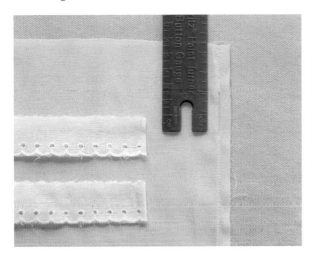

6. With the right sides together and the raw edges of the trim even with the raw top edge of the outer bag, baste the trim to the top of the bag using a scant 1/4" (6mm) seam.

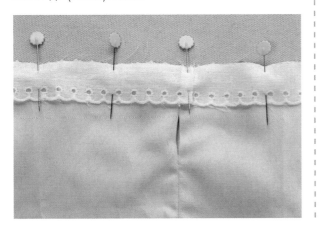

7. With right sides together, place the outer bag into the lining (the outside of the lining will be facing you). With the top edges of the bag and the lining even, stitch around the top of the bag through all layers. Pull the outer bag through the opening in the lining. Turn in the edges of the lining opening, and machine-sew the opening closed. Turn the lining to the inside, and press the top edge of the bag, pulling the trim up.

8. To make the casing for the ties, find the 2 openings you left in the side seams. With the outside of the bag facing you, at the ends of the openings, stitch 2 straight rows, 1" (2.5cm) apart, through both layers of fabric. These rows should be parallel to each other and to the top of the bag.

9. To run the ties through the casing, attach a large safety pin to one end of one piece of the ribbon. Feed the ribbon through the casing, across the front of the bag, and out the opposite side opening. Repeat for the other tie on the back of the bag. Pull the ties to draw the bag closed, and make bows out of the 2 ties on each side.

TIP:
* White seems like white, until you hold it up to another white and discover just how many shades of white there are. It's unlikely that your white embroidery floss will match the whites of the eyelet trim you choose, but don't get hung up on it. If anything, choose trims with matching shades, and let the embroidery color differ slightly.

This sweet gingham ring pillow with an embroidered covered button would be perfect at a country wedding. It couldn't be simpler to make, and can be completely personalized in the wedding colors and with any monogram. Small designs are perfect for covered buttons. If the wedding has a particular theme or motif, transfer that onto the fabric and make this unique gift for the special couple.

MATERIALS

Heart Button Ring Pillow template (page 156)

For the pillow: Two 8 1/2" x 8 1/2" (21.5cm x 21.5 cm) pieces of gingham dupioni silk, cut on the bias

For the button cover: One 6" x 6" (15cm x 15cm) piece of fine-weave linen

For the strap (on back): 5" (12.5cm) of 1/2" (13mm) ribbon

For the tie: 18" (45.5cm) of 1/2" (13mm) ribbon

One 1 7/8" (4.8cm) self-covered button form

4" (10cm) embroidery hoop

Micron marker or fabric marker

Embroidery floss

Polyester fiberfill or wool batting

FINISHED SIZE

8" x 8" (20.5cm x 20.5 cm)

SEAM ALLOWANCE

1/4" (6mm), unless otherwise noted

1. To make the button, copy the Heart Button template and draw a monogram in the center of the heart by hand, or use your computer to create a simple initial. Transfer the design to the center of the button fabric. Embroider using 2 strands of embroidery floss with chain stitch, laced back stitch, lazy daisy stitch, and French knots. (See Embroidery [page 134].) Centering design, cut fabric into a 3" (7.5cm) circle.

2. To cover the button, using a running stitch, sew evenly around the circle about $^1/8$" (3mm) from the edge (see Hand-sewing [page 130]). Place a button form in the center of the circle of fabric (with the front of the button facing the wrong side of the fabric), and pull stitches to cinch the fabric

around the button evenly. Check placement of the embroidery on the front of the button before attaching the back of the button securely, following the manufacturer's instructions.

3. To make the hand strap for the back, turn under $^1/4$" (6mm) on each end of the strap ribbon piece and press. Center the ribbon horizontally on the right side of the pillow back piece. Machine-stitch the folded ends of ribbon to the pillow back. (Use a shorter ribbon if your ring bearer has a tiny hand.)

4. Place the pillow pieces right sides together, and stitch around all 4 sides, leaving a 2" (5cm) opening in one side of the pillow. Clip the corners and turn the pillow right side out. Stuff the pillow lightly with fiberfill. Turn in the edges of the opening and slip stitch closed (see Hand-sewing [page 130]).

5. Stitch the button to center of the pillow tightly, through all layers, burying the tails in the body of the pillow (see Hand-sewing [page 130]). Tie the ribbon around the button and thread each ring into the ribbon bow. Now say, "I do!"

TIP:
* Don't overstuff your pillow or the button will get surrounded by stuffing when it gets tied in. Keep the pillow evenly stuffed so that it's unwrinkled but still very squishy.

wedding guestbook wall hanging

Ten years after our wedding, when I looked at the guestbook signed by our family and friends, I felt really emotional seeing everyone's handwriting. The signatures were so familiar to me: my grandma's, from every birthday card; my college roommate's, from every notebook she had filled up and all our letters since; a friend's daughter who'd just learned to write. Today, some of the people live far from me; others have passed away. But their signatures feel as evocative as photographs. Making handwritten names permanent with embroidery floss is a beautiful way to honor each signer's presence at our wedding and in our life.

MATERIALS
Wedding Guestbook Wall Hanging template (page 153)
One photo, sized at 6" x 6" (15cm x 15cm) and 200 dpi
For photo heart patch: One 8 1/2" x 11" (21.5cm x 28cm) ink-jet printer–ready fabric sheet
For the foundation: One 18" x 16" (45.5cm x 40.5cm) piece of muslin

For the interlining: One 19" x 17" (48.5cm x 43cm) piece of Timtex
For the backing: One 19" x 17" (48.5cm x 43cm) piece of jacquard or embroidered cotton (something fancy)
For the binding: 2 yd (1.8m) of 1" (2.5cm) binding
One 8 1/2" x 11" (21.5cm x 28cm) piece of heat-resistant template plastic

Dressmaker's chalk
Micron marker or fabric marker
Embroidery floss in black and dark gray, and 2 shades of contrasting colors (like pink and dark pink)
4" (10cm) embroidery hoop
Tape maker, 1" (2.5cm) size
Spray starch

FINISHED SIZE
18" x 16" (45.5cm x 40.5cm)

1. To prepare the heart patch, trace the Heart template onto a piece of heat-resistant template plastic. Cut the heart out of the plastic. Using your computer, resize a wedding photo to 6" x 6" (15cm x 15cm), centering the bride and groom so that they will be within the stitching line of the Heart template. Print the photo onto the ink-jet printer–ready fabric, and heat-set (see Transferring Photos to Fabric [page 133]).

2. Place the Heart template over the photo, centering the bride and groom. Trace around the heart with dressmaker's chalk, and cut it out adding a 1/4" [6mm] seam allowance. Following the instructions in Appliqué (page 137), prepare the heart to be attached to the foundation piece

by clipping, applying starch, and pressing edges under. Pin the heart in place on the foundation piece, and attach it using a slip stitch (see Hand-Sewing [page 130]). Transfer the small dots from the Heart template to the foundation piece.

3. To prepare the signatures, photocopy the pages from your guestbook at 150 percent. Cut out the individual signatures and lay them under the foundation piece in a pleasing arrangement. Trace the signatures onto the muslin, using the fabric marker or, ideally, a fine-tip Micron marker. (You will get a more detailed line with the Micron, but it is permanent, so use it with caution.) Using the embroidery hoop and one strand of embroidery floss, embroider the signatures with back stitches,

alternating black and dark gray among the names to lend variety and texture. Using 2 strands of embroidery floss, at the small dots around the heart-shaped photo on the foundation piece, stitch

French knots in alternating colors (see Embroidery [page 134]).

4. When all the embroidery is completed, carefully press the foundation piece, removing all the wrinkles left by the embroidery hoop. Place the backing fabric, right side down, on the work surface. Lay the Timtex on top of the backing fabric, and the foundation piece, right side up, on top of the Timtex. The bottom layers are a bit larger than the foundation piece so that it is easier to keep all the layers lined up when basting. Pin around all the edges and baste through all layers, a scant 1/4" (6mm) from the edge. Trim the edges of the Timtex and backing fabric even with the foundation piece.

5. Using the instructions in General Sewing Techniques (page 125), make the binding and apply around the edge of the wall hanging.

6. To make the stitches by which the piece will hang, using 2 strands of embroidery floss, make a knotless start (see Hand-Sewing [page 130]) on the back of the piece in an upper corner, securing the thread to the Timtex and backing only (don't sew through to the front). Make a 1/2" (13mm) stitch, running the needle back under the Timtex and backing only, coming up where you started. Repeat the 1/2" (13mm) stitch and fasten off, burying the tails of the floss (see Hand-Sewing [page 130]) under the backing and snipping off the ends. Repeat for the opposite upper corner.

TIPS:

* After I completed this project, I realized that I should've included my signature and my husband's and our wedding date. When you make this, you might want to add those elements.

* If the wedding hasn't happened yet, you're in luck. When it does, make sure attendees know where the guestbook is and sign it. Get the bridal party to sign, and the parents of the bride and groom. Oftentimes, the people who are closest to the action are too busy to pay attention to the guestbook, but I'd now give anything to have my dad's signature in ours.

APPENDICES

General Sewing Techniques

To complete the projects in this book, it is helpful to understand a few of the sewing techniques I've used to achieve my results.

PREPARING FABRICS

If you're going to be washing your finished project, you'll want to prewash the fabric (unless specifically instructed not to) to remove sizing and to preshrink the material so your beautiful finished piece won't pucker the first time you launder it. Trim a $1/2$" (13mm) triangle off each corner of your fabric to prevent a chaos of raveled, tangled threads upon removal from either washer or dryer (it really works!). Don't use fabric softener or dryer sheets.

If you'll be incorporating vintage fabric in your projects, wash it by hand, and lay it in the sun to dry or flat on a towel indoors if it's raining. To help remove stains and musty odors, I brew an elixir of 1 cup Cascade (powdered dishwasher detergent), 1 cup baking soda, 1 cup sea salt, and 1 cup vinegar in about 4 gallons of water in a clean bathtub, and let my vintage fabrics soak for up to a day. Rinse the fabrics well, until the water runs clear, because detergent left in fabrics can yellow with time.

Press out wrinkles and folds in fabrics, using your iron's recommended settings and a spray bottle of water. It takes extra time, but consider it your bonding, getting-to-know-you phase. It tests your patience and it's awkward, yes (it's not easy to press big, uncut pieces of fabric), but it's worth it in the long run, as in any good relationship.

USING TEMPLATES

Templates are provided in this book for projects that require you to cut particular shapes. To use the templates, simply enlarge them on a copy machine to the percentage specified, and cut them out, adding seam allowances as indicated in individual pattern directions. Place the template right side down on the wrong side of the fabric, noting the grain or edge to be placed on the fold, and trace around the shape with dressmaker's chalk or a fabric marker as indicated. Be sure to trace all symbols.

MITERING A CORNER

When two hemmed edges meet at a right angle, the prettiest way to join the edges is to create a mitered corner. Trimming and folding a corner in this way reduces bulk and gives you a tidy finish.

1. With the fabric wrong side up, turn in $1/4$" (6mm) of each edge and press. Then fold in each edge again along hemlines (the dotted lines in the drawing, below). Press, then unfold only the second set of folds.

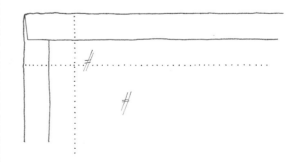

2. Turn down the corner so the edges are parallel with the hemlines and the corner fold lies diagonally across the intersection of the hemlines.

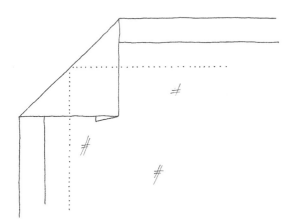

3. Trim off the corner, leaving a $^1/_4$" (6mm) allowance. Fold in the edges along the hemlines.

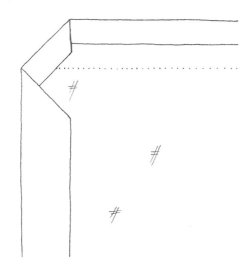

4. Slip stitch the edges of the mitered corner together (see Hand-Sewing [page 130]). Sew the turned edges of the hems either by hand, with hemstitch or slip stitch, or by machine.

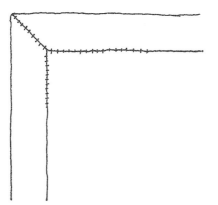

CLIPPING CURVES AND TRIMMING CORNERS

Clipping curves and trimming corners reduces the amount of fabric left in the seam and results in a smoother, neater finish. With sharp scissors, make small cuts at intervals around curves, snipping almost to but not through the seam. On curves that will be turned inward, clip wedges to further reduce bulk. On corners (or points), trim across the point, almost to but not through the seam.

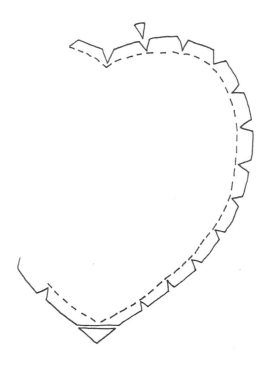

MAKING AND ATTACHING BINDING

To me, there is no lovelier way to finish the raw edges on a quilt, wall hanging, or stocking than with machine-and-hand-stitched binding.

If you're binding something with straight edges and mitered corners, straight grain–cut binding works just fine. Bias tape—binding that is cut on the bias—is great if the edge you're trying to bind is curvy and needs the flexibility that a bias cut affords. Ready-made bias tape can be purchased prepackaged or by the yard at fabric stores, and this is convenient for projects that don't require a fussy binding since it comes in a limited number of colors, widths, and fiber contents.

But if you want more control over this decorative element of your project, you may want to make your own binding with the help of a rotary cutter, clear-plastic ruler, self-healing cutting mat, and a handy little gadget called a tape maker, available in several sizes at any fabric store. Tape makers require you to cut strips of fabric that are double the width of the tape you are trying to achieve, join them together, feed the strip through the gadget, and press the folds as they are created by the tool. Complete instructions on cutting strips for, joining, and making tape are included when you purchase your tape maker.

Preferences vary when it comes to attaching binding. The quickest way is to simply slip the folded binding over the raw edge of the item, pin, then machine sew close to the edge of the binding but still catching the underside in the seam. When binding a quilt or something with straight edges and corners, you can always use strips of fabric folded lengthwise with wrong sides together. Align the raw edges of the binding with the top edge of the quilt and stitch through all layers, $1/4"$ (6mm) from the edge. Then turn the binding to the back and hand-sew the folded edge down, covering the seam and using a slip stitch. This will give you a double layer of fabric over the edges, making it nice and durable.

But my favorite way of making and attaching binding, even on quilts, is to use the tape maker to fold the strips, then attach them by machine and by hand. I think I just like using the tape maker.

Making tape

1. Cut strips of fabric twice as wide as the tape maker's small end, either on the straight grain or bias, depending on your project.

2. To join straight grain–cut strips, stitch ends right sides together using a $1/4"$ (6mm) seam. To join bias-cut strips, cut the ends at a 45-degree angle and place them, right sides together, perpendicular to each other.

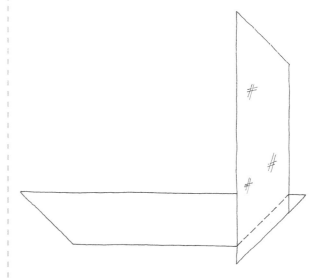

3. Stitch the seam. Press the seam open, and trim the corners to be even with the strip. When your strip is long enough, feed it, wrong side up, into the tape maker (to create folds), and it will come out the other end of the gadget. Press the tape flat.

Attaching double-fold binding by machine and by hand-sewing.

1. With the right side of the tape facing the right side of the fabric, match the raw edge of the unfolded tape to the raw edge of the fabric, and pin along the fold line. Stitch along the fold line.

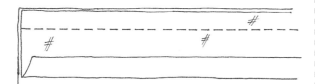

2. Turn the binding to the wrong side of the fabric, enclosing the raw edge. Hand-sew the folded edge down with a hemstitch or slip stitch (see Hand-Sewing [page 130]).

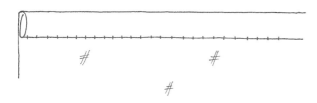

Turning a corner with binding.

1. Stitch along the fold line of the binding almost to the corner, stopping and making a few back stitches at the point where the perpendicular seam line will cross.

2. Fold the binding diagonally, so it is now perpendicular to the seam.

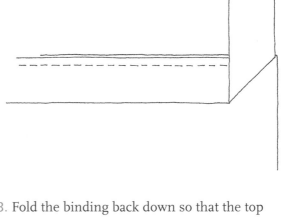

3. Fold the binding back down so that the top fold is aligned with the binding edge. Pin and machine stitch, starting and backstitching a bit, right at the folded edge through all layers.

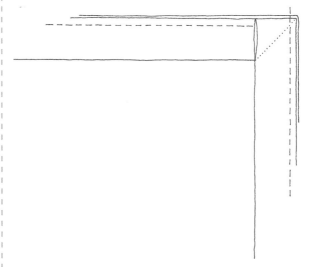

4. Fold the binding over the raw edges to the back of the piece, forming neat miters on the front and back, and slip stitch the mitered edges closed. Slip stitch the folded edge down, covering the seam.

MAKING YO-YOS

To make a yo-yo, cut a circle of fabric with a diameter twice that of the finished yo-yo plus $^1/_4$" (6mm). Knot a length of heavyweight thread at one end. Turn under a $^1/_4$" (6mm) hem with your fingers while making a row of running stitches through both thicknesses around the edge of the circle. Pull the thread tight to gather up the circle, making a little pouch. Secure the thread with a few stitches at the beginning of the seam.

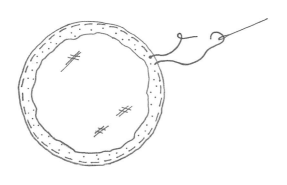

FELTING A WOOL SWEATER

Remove the sleeves at the shoulder seams, and slit open the sleeve seam (to help eliminate permanent creases). Machine-wash the sweater in hot water with enough detergent to give you a fair amount of suds. Throw in a pair of old jeans to increase the agitation and help the sweater to felt. Rinse in cold water, and dry on medium-high heat. You may need to wash and dry the sweater a second time to achieve the degree of felting you want.

MAKING A SQUARE BOTTOM

Making a square bottom on a bag is one of those things that's easier to do than to explain. Once you get the hang of it, though, you'll see there's nothing to it.

1. With the right sides of the bag pieces together, machine-sew the side and bottom seams of the bag.

2. Keeping the wrong side out and the side seam facing you, stick your hand into the bag, toward one corner. With your other hand, push the side seam flat, pressing it against the bottom seam, creating a point with the corner of the bag as its apex. (Remove your hand from the bag.)

3. Keeping the side seam flat against the bottom seam, measure the required distance from the point and draw a line across the corner, perpendicular to the side seam.

4. Machine-sew across the corner on the line. Repeat all steps for the opposite corner of the bag. Turn the bag right side out and push the points toward the bottom center of the bag.

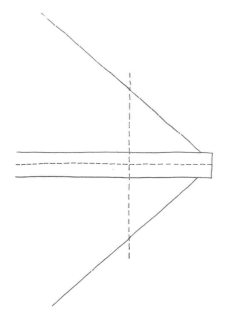

To complete several of the projects in this book, you will occasionally need to work some basic stitches by hand. Closing openings, attaching binding and appliqué, and working on dolls all require the precision and delicacy that you can only achieve with hand-sewing. Personally, I love stitching things by hand. Never am I happier than when faced with a new DVD, a cup of hot cocoa, and a whole lot of binding to attach by hand.

Make sure you have a nice, new, sharp needle. It sounds obvious, but you'd be surprised how frustrating it can be to stitch things by hand with a dull needle. Hand-sewing needles come in a wide variety of sizes and lengths. The higher the size number, the smaller the needle diameter. Generally, you'll want to use the smallest needle possible for the job (a big needle may leave a hole in your fabric), but most of all you want to find a needle that's comfortable for you. It's worth a little experimentation to find the type you like. Some of the projects call for a heavyweight (like upholstery) thread, which requires a bigger needle. And some, like the Nutcracker Doll, require you to sew strands of yarn through the doll to create hair; in this case, needles called "yarn darners"—very sharp and wide—are necessary. A thimble or a rubber finger protector comes in handy, too, for pushing the needle through the fabric.

Consider purchasing a full-spectrum light source. Available at any craft or fabric store, full-spectrum lamps allow you to see your work as if you were viewing it in bright daylight. This kind of light can be invaluable when you're choosing colors or working detailed areas that strain your eyes.

Hand-sewing might not have the star quality of some of the flashier techniques in your repertoire, but when done carefully and correctly, it has a quiet beauty that can really make the difference in the quality of your finished piece. Below are some hand-sewing techniques you will need to know.

RUNNING STITCH

This simple stitch travels forward in a back-and-forth motion. It can be used for embroidery, as well. Working from right to left, weave the point of the needle in and out of fabric, then pull the thread through. To gather fabric, make running stitches along the seam to be gathered, then pull up the thread at each end, bunching up the fabric between the stitches.

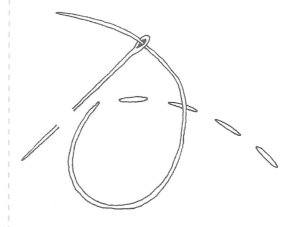

BASTING STITCH

Used to temporarily shape or hold pieces together, this stitch is like the running stitch, but longer. Leave ends unknotted so that these stitches will be easy to remove.

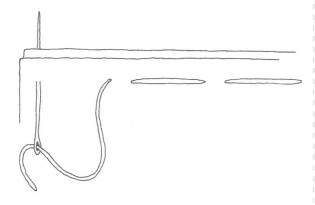

BACK STITCH

This sturdy stitch is used to join seams together, and is also used to create linework in embroidery. Working from right to left, sew a long stitch forward, underneath the fabric, and a shorter stitch backward into the end of the previous stitch.

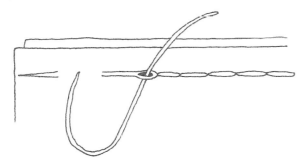

HEMSTITCH

I like to use this stitch to attach binding to a thick piece of fabric, like felt, or a project with layers in which the thread can be hidden. Working from right to left, bring the needle and thread through the hem edge. Make a tiny stitch, catching only a couple of threads of the front of the piece. Then slide the needle under the hem about $1/4$" (6mm) to the left, just catching the hem above the fold.

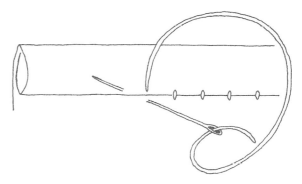

SLIP STITCH

This stitch is practically invisible, so it works well when attaching a folded edge to a single layer of fabric. Working from right to left, make a tiny stitch in the main fabric, catching only a few threads. Opposite this stitch, insert the needle into the folded edge of the hem, and run it along the fold for about $1/4$" (6mm). Bring the needle out, drawing the thread through.

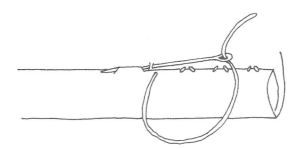

WHIPSTITCH

I like to use a whipstitch to attach stuffed parts of toys together. Insert the needle from the back edge to the front. Keep the needle at a diagonal to move from right to left along the seam.

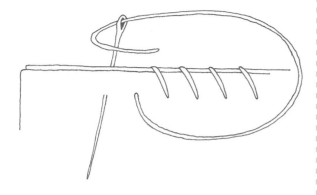

BLANKET STITCH

The blanket stitch is both decorative and functional. It can be used to join pieces of fabric together or to finish a raw or folded edge. To start the stitch, the thread is anchored and brought up just below the top edge of the fabric. Then insert the needle the same distance below the edge as the stitch is wide. Bring the needle up behind the fabric, looping the thread around the back of the needle to form the top ridge.

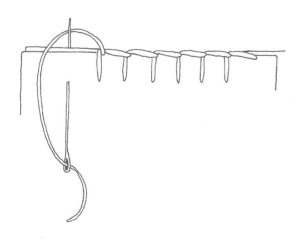

KNOTLESS START

This is a great way to start stitching on anything that doesn't have a "back," or where you don't want to use a knot. Simply fold the length of thread you are going to use in half, with the 2 cut ends even. Thread those ends through the eye of the needle, leaving the folded end long. Begin sewing by pushing the needle into the front of your fabric and, without pulling the thread all the way through the fabric, take a small stitch, coming up just $1/16"$ (1.5mm) away from where you went in. Pull the needle out through the loop created by the folded end of the thread and pull firmly to secure.

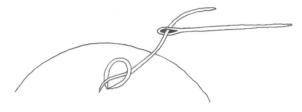

BURYING TAILS

To finish off a line of hand-stitching in a piece that is stuffed or layered, make a small knot at the end of your last stitch. Push the needle into the fabric near the knot, then poke it back up through the fabric about an inch (2.5cm) away from where you went in. Pull the needle tautly, pushing the knot through the fabric to the inside. Trim the thread tail close to the fabric top and maneuver the thread so it is pulled back inside the piece and is invisible.

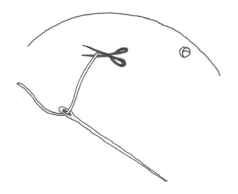

Though there are many ways to transfer photos and other original documents (drawings, diplomas, letters, etc.) to fabric, the way that I prefer involves nothing more than an ink-jet printer and specially prepared 8 1/2" x 11" (21.5cm x 28cm) fabric sheets, easily purchased online or at any fabric store. These fabric sheets are typically made of finely woven white or cream-colored fabric and have a paper stiffener attached to them for easy feeding into your printer. They've also been treated so that they are washable, dry-cleanable, and colorfast. **Be sure** to check the details on the packages of fabric you purchase as there are many types of finishes, weaves, and treatments available.

If the expense of these is prohibitive (and you will be paying for convenience here) or you just want to use your own fabric to get a particular "look," you can also print on your own (finely woven) fabric by treating it with bubble-jet setter (available at craft and fabric stores [see Resources, page 143] and cutting it to 8 1/2" x 11" (21.5cm x 28cm). Then just smooth it onto a full sheet of sticker paper, available at office supply stores. (Some people suggest using freezer paper to stabilize the fabric during the printing process, but I find it to be too soft, which can lead to printer jams . . . or worse [permanent printer jams].) Comprehensive directions for treating your own fabric with these products are given on their packaging.

When choosing photos or images to transfer, the quality of your original counts. Pick photos that "read" well and have good contrast, and avoid images that appear blurry or have areas that are complicated. You will only lose information during the transfer process, so for best results, choose originals that can sacrifice a bit of sharpness and still look good. Photo-editing software can turn up the volume on old photos by increasing contrast and sharpening soft lines. If you're scanning documents or images, make sure that your files are printing out at about 200 dpi (dots per inch [2.5cm]) at the dimensions you need for your project. Most home ink-jet printers print at about 150 dpi, but I like to keep the resolution of my images a bit higher, just in case I need to resize. Consult your photo-editing software manual for information on scanning and resizing photos.

A little experimentation is helpful when printing photos to fabric, since each printer is different, and fabric content and weave vary widely. Typically, you will set your printer to the "plain" paper setting. Increasing print quality here will only result in too much ink being deposited on the fabric, which doesn't absorb ink the same way paper does. After printing, allow the ink to dry. Then rinse the fabric under cold water until it runs clear. Heat-set the ink with a warm iron, using a press cloth to absorb any excess ink and to protect your image. Easy!

Decorative embroidery is one of the sweetest and most gratifying techniques you can use to personalize special projects. It's been around since the dawn of time, and it's as charming today as it's ever been. The plethora of fonts on your computer and any basic word processing or design software allows you to easily make monograms, spell out words, and create numbers to embroider, based on your whim. And centering and resizing? No problem!

Before you embroider, consider your fabric. Even-weave cotton and linen work best, since they have the same number of threads going crosswise and lengthwise. An even weave helps minimize distortion as fabric is pushed and pulled around. Certain projects, like the Snail Onesie, direct you to apply an iron-on stabilizer to the back of a stretchy knit fabric, which can make it easier to work stitches on the front.

To transfer designs to fabric, you must first have your design printed out at the desired size. If you're creating text using your computer, consider using fonts and sizes of type that are both easy to stitch and easy to read. Then press your fabric so that it is smooth.

My preferred method of transferring a design to cotton or linen fabric is to use a light box (a bright window works, too) and a fine-tip fabric or permanent marker to trace shapes directly onto my fabric. Using masking tape,

tape your design, right side up, to the light source, then attach your fabric securely on top of the design with more tape, and trace the entire image before moving anything.

I use a Micron 01 (.25mm) for almost every design I transfer. This very fine-tip permanent drawing marker, available at art supply stores, works well for large designs, since the line it makes is easy to cover but it won't disappear in a couple of days as some fabric markers are typically engineered to do. (Some markers say they'll stay visible until you wash them out, which is nice, but they can sometimes fade before you're finished.) Just make sure your line is fine enough to be easily covered by your thread if you're using permanent ink.

You can also use dressmaker's carbon to transfer the design to heavyweight fabrics, like felt, or garments like a onesie. Lay the carbon sheet carbon side down on the garment, and then lay your design on top, and trace the design with a ballpoint pen, pressing firmly. Alternatively, print out your design in reverse, and trace it with an embroidery-transfer pencil onto a piece of tracing paper. Then you can iron the tracing directly onto your fabric, creating permanent markings. Oftentimes you can get more than one transfer out of the tracing as well, which makes this method convenient if you are making more than one or repeating a design element.

All these methods work. Just decide which you prefer for your project's particular needs.

Many of the stitches found in the Hand-Sewing appendix can be done with embroidery threads, but here are a few more you might want to use.

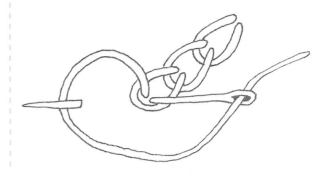

SATIN STITCH

This stitch is used to fill areas with long, smooth stitches, providing an elegant, shimmery finish. Stitches should be worked smoothly from one edge to the other, and laid close together so no fabric shows through.

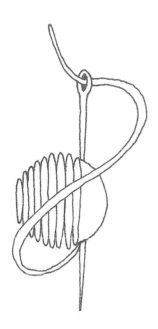

FRENCH KNOT

The French knot can be used for small embroidered details and to dot the "i"s when writing in thread. Some people find this stitch tricky to learn, but just remember to hold the thread taut with your other hand as you pull the needle through.

Bring the needle up through the fabric where you want the knot to be. Holding the needle in your right hand, wrap the thread around the needle clockwise twice. Insert the needle into the fabric close to where it just emerged. Holding the thread tight against the needle with your left thumb and forefinger, pull the needle and thread through the knot gently.

CHAIN STITCH

Chain stitch is made by working a chain of loops in a line, with each link starting and ending in the link previous. To work it, bring the needle up through the fabric. Holding the thread down with your hand opposite the one holding the needle, insert the needle close to where it emerged. Bring the point out a short distance away and loop the thread under the point of the needle. Pull the needle out, and continue each link of the chain in the same way.

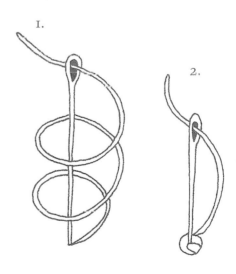

LAZY DAISY STITCH

The lazy daisy stitch is often one of the first decorative stitches that children learn and is similar to the chain stitch. To work it, push the needle into the fabric at the base of the petal, and bring it up at the top of the petal. Loop the thread under the point of the needle and pull the needle all the way through the fabric. Make a small vertical stitch across the thread at the top of the petal to secure.

LACED BACK STITCH

To make a line of backstitches a bit more interesting, a contrast color of thread can be woven back and forth from one side of the line to the other. The lacing is done when the backstitching is complete and does not pass through the fabric at all (except to start it, of course). Use a blunt-ended needle to make it easier to pass the thread under the stitches; a sharper needle can get caught on the fabric or existing embroidery.

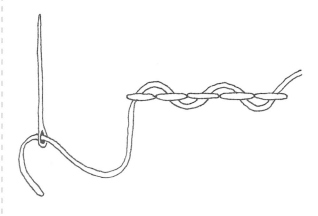

Appliqué

Appliqué is a technique in which small fabric shapes (usually 100 percent cotton) are arranged and then sewn onto a foundation piece of fabric. There are different ways to approach appliqué, and each gives a distinct look to your finished piece, from raw to finished. The method you choose should depend on how much time you have and the overall look you want to achieve.

If you're in a hurry, or going for a more rustic look, the simplest way to appliqué is just to cut some shapes, leave their edges raw, pin them in place, and stitch them onto the foundation fabric, either by machine or with simple running stitches done by hand. This will give you an edgy, frizzy finish, and for some projects this feels just right.

A nice way to handle complicated pieces, like the tree in the Family Tree project, is to apply double-sided fusible web (following the manufacturer's instructions) to your shape, then iron it directly onto the foundation piece. You can then go around the edge of the shape with a small machine zigzag stitch, or trim it by hand with a blanket stitch. This type of application will give you a flat look.

My favorite type of appliqué has turned-under edges and is stitched to the foundation piece by hand. It's an old-fashioned look that you'll see on many antique quilts. This method will give your fabric shapes a finished edge, and will make them appear slightly raised when stitched to the foundation fabric.

To prepare turned-edge pieces in the traditional way, you will need a piece of heat-resistant template plastic (available in the quilting section of craft and fabric stores) and

a pair of not-your-best scissors for cutting plastic. To create a template, simply place the plastic over the pattern for the piece. Trace the shape with a fine-tip permanent marker, and then cut out the shape on the traced line.

Place the template right side down on the wrong side of the fabric. Trace around the template with a fabric marker, and then trim the fabric (with your good scissors this time) around the shape, $1/4$" (6mm) outside the line. Around the edge of the shape, clip curves almost to—but not through—the traced line. If any part of your piece will be overlapped by another, don't bother clipping (or, ultimately, turning) that edge. Just leave it flat, and the other piece will cover it when you assemble the design.

On a protected surface, spray a bit of liquid spray starch into a small bowl. Place the plastic template wrong side up on the wrong side of the fabric piece and, using a small paintbrush, dab liquid starch around the edges of the pieces that are to be turned. Then press the edges of the fabric over the template edges with the tip of a hot iron, or with an appliqué iron if your piece is really small. Make small tucks in the fabric when going around outside curves, and overlap clipped edges when smoothing through inside curves. For points, press excess fabric directly over the tip of the template, then fold in the edges and press to miter the corner (see Hand-Sewing [page 130]).

After pressing the turned edges around the plastic template, turn the piece over and press the front. Allow the plastic to cool, then gently remove the template from the piece. Stitch the piece onto the foundation fabric using a sharp needle, polyester thread, and a slip stitch (see Hand-Sewing [page 130]). Alternatively, you could use a blanket stitch and embroidery floss for an old-fashioned look.

For some simple shapes, another technique that works well is to turn the edges by sewing the appliqué piece to another piece of lightweight fabric, like muslin. Place the appliqué fabric and the lining together with right sides facing. Trace the shape (with its wrong side facing you) onto the wrong side of the lining. Machine stitch around the shape on the traced line. Trim the seam close to the stitching, clipping curves and trimming points. Cut a slit in the lining and turn the shape right side out. Press, and attach to the foundation piece.

To turn a beautifully smooth circle, do not clip the edge of the shape. Instead, knot a length of thread and work a running stitch between the plastic template and the edge of the fabric. Pull the thread to gather excess fabric and smooth puckers evenly around the edge of the circle. Secure with a small stitch, add starch to the edges, and press.

Experiment with these techniques to find the method and the look that you prefer. I like to use a few different types of appliqué together on the same project for a textured, more interesting look.

Freezer-Paper Stenciling

Freezer-paper stenciling is an easy, inexpensive way to transfer simple images or letters to fabric: You simply use this special paper, an iron, and a bit of fabric paint. Freezer paper has a waxy residue that, when ironed, temporarily bonds to fabric. When cut into a stencil, the bond creates a sealed silhouette inside of which you can paint. Freezer paper is available in rolls at the grocery store, or, more conveniently (though expensively, but well worth it, in my mind) in flat, printable sheets at the craft or fabric store.

To make a freezer-paper stencil, size your image on a computer or a copier to 100 percent. Print it out on regular white paper just as you want it to appear on your fabric. Lay the printed image on a hard surface, and place a piece of freezer paper—waxy side down—over the top. On the freezer paper, trace your image with a pencil or marker, then cut away all parts of the image you want to fill with color. (Keep the floating pieces intact, like the inside of an "o"; you will use these when assembling the stencil.) If your image has large areas, you may want to use sharp, pointed embroidery scissors; otherwise use an X-acto knife on a self-healing cutting board for finely detailed areas.

Heat your iron to the setting that corresponds to the type of fabric you are using. Place your stencil, waxy side down, on the right side of your fabric. Gently iron the freezer paper to the fabric, checking to make sure the paper has had time to stick but not long enough to scorch the fabric. Then place any of the floating pieces in their correct positions and iron those on, too.

Fabric paint is pigment mixed with a gluelike binder; it sticks well to almost any kind of fabric. For the projects in this book, you can use any water-soluble, iron-to-set fabric paint. Place a few paper towels under your fabric.

To apply the paint, use a paintbrush or a stenciling brush—go slowly and do several light coats, paying special attention to the corners of your image. Let it set for a few hours, until the paint is completely dry. Then peel your stencil off and heat-set the paint with your iron and a press cloth (again, use the heat setting that corresponds to the type of fabric you've painted). Once it's heat-set, you can use, wear, or launder your stenciled fabric. Cool, huh?

Glossary

To brush up on your sewing lingo, here are some common terms, and their definitions:

backstitch: To make a few stitches backward over the previous stitches to secure the beginning or end of a seam. Also a type of embroidery stitch used to outline shapes or write text.

baste: To sew with long stitches to temporarily hold one or more pieces of fabric together. Basting stitches are usually removed later.

batting: The layer of insulation between a quilt top and back, available at fabric stores in various lofts and fibers.

bias: The line going diagonally across the straight grain of a length of fabric. To cut something "on the bias" means to place the grainline of the template you are cutting at a 45-degree angle to the fabric selvage.

bias tape: Strips of fabric cut on the bias, turned under, pressed, and applied as bindings where there is a need for stretch around curves.

binding: Encasing the raw edges of a quilt or garment with another piece of fabric. The fabric that is folded and used to encase the raw edges is also called "binding"; binding is also called "tape."

burying tails: After knotting off, pulling the ends of the thread into the body of a stuffed or layered item and snipping them off as they emerge.

clipping: Cutting into the seam allowance perpendicular to (but not through) the sewn seam, allowing the fabric to lie flat around curves.

dpi: Dots per square inch (2.5cm); a measure of resolution.

dressmaker's carbon paper: A paper with a special surface that allows marks to be transferred to fabric traced over (pressing firmly) with a pencil or a tracing wheel.

eyelet trim: Cotton fabric or trim decorated with holes, embroidered around the edges.

freezer paper: Paper with a special residue on one side that temporarily bonds to fabric when ironed.

French seam: A seam stitched first with the wrong sides together, then turned in and stitched with the right sides together, so the raw edges are enclosed within the seam.

fusible web: A stiff material with an adhesive coating on one side that adheres to fabric when heated, giving body and stability to your piece (available in both single- and double-sided versions).

gather: To run a row of loose stitches along the edge of a piece of fabric, allowing you to pull excess fabric into a seam line. This creates the puckered look of gathers.

grain: The direction that threads are woven in a fabric. Lengthwise grain runs the length of the fabric from cut edge to cut edge; crosswise grain runs from selvage to selvage.

gusset: A panel of fabric added to provide ease of movement or dimension.

knotless start: A method to secure thread when stitching items that don't have an actual "back."

miter: To join two edges at a 45-degree angle, typically done to finish a corner smoothly.

muslin: Lightweight plain-woven cotton fabric used as lining or to make trial-run garments for fitting

pinking shears: Shears with a zigzag or scalloped edge, used decoratively or to prevent unfinished fabric edges from fraying.

pivot: When machine-sewing, to stop, leaving the needle in the "down" position, raising the presser foot and turning the fabric sharply before lowering the foot and continuing to sew, usually around a corner.

pressing cloth: A piece of clean, white, lint-free cotton fabric placed between the iron and the garment to prevent possible scorching on delicate fabrics.

raw edge: The unfinished edge of the fabric.

seam allowance: The amount of fabric left between the line of stitching (the seam) and the edge of the fabric.

selvage: The finished edge of the fabric as it comes off the bolt.

stabilizer: A rigid fabric interlining that restricts the stretch of selected areas of the piece.

stitch in the ditch: Stitching in or a few threads away from an already stitched seam.

template: A shape used as a guide when cutting fabric, often made of paper or plastic.

topstitch: A row of stitching near the seam but on the outside of the finished piece; generally decorative.

Resources

I am lucky enough to live in a city that boasts many brick-and-mortar fabric and craft stores, and I buy the majority of my supplies from people I know and shops that have for years welcomed my slow crawls up and down their aisles, searching for the perfect thing. But the myriad on-line retailers specializing in gorgeous fabrics, notions, books, buttons, and everything in between have truly made the craft world a world without borders. This list will help you find sources for some of the harder-to-find materials I've used in my projects, and point you toward some of my favorite shops on-line, as well as some other resources that you may find useful.

NEW FABRICS, NOTIONS, AND SUPPLIES

Cia's Palette
612–229–5227
www.ciaspalette.com

Fabric Depot
700 SE 122nd Avenue
Portland, OR 97233
888–896–1478
www.fabricdepot.com

Jo-Ann Fabric and Crafts
www.joann.com

Mill End Store
9701 SE McLoughlin Blvd.
Portland, OR 97222
503–786–1234
www.millendstore.com

Purl Patchwork
147 Sullivan Street
New York, NY 10012
212–420–8798
www.purlsoho.com

Reprodepot Fabrics
877–738–7632
www.reprodepotfabrics.com

Sew-Biz Fabrics
www.sewbizfabrics.com

EQuilter.com
5455 Spine Road, Suite E
Boulder, CO 80301
877-FABRIC-3
www.eQuilter.com

Primrose Design
www.primrosedesign.com

VINTAGE FABRICS

Pamela Simon Vintage Fabrics
101 N. Main St.
Ambler, PA 19002
215 540 1920
www.psvintage.com

Revival Fabrics
www.revivalfabrics.com

Sharon's Vintage Fabrics
www.rickrack.com

SPECIAL NOTIONS AND MILLINERY SUPPLIES

The Button Emporium
914 SW 11th Avenue
Portland, OR 97205
503–228–6372
www.buttonemporium.com

Dolls and Lace
P.O. Box 743
Lehi, Utah 84043
801–836–8769
www.dollsandlace.com

Papier Valise
403–277–1802
www.papiervalise.com

Tinsel Trading
47 W. 38th Street
New York, NY 10018
212–730–1030
www.tinseltrading.com

WOOL FELT

A Child's Dream Come True
1223-D Michigan Street
Sandpoint, ID 83864
800–359–2906
www.achildsdream.com

Magic Cabin
888–623–3655
www.magiccabin.com

National Nonwovens
P.O. Box 150
Easthampton, MA 01027
800–333–3469
www.nationalnonwovens.com

INK-JET PRINTER–READY FABRIC

Blumenthal Craft
1929 Main Street
Lansing, IA 52151
563–538–4211
www.blumenthallansing.com

The Electric Quilt Company
419 Gould Street #2
Bowling Green, OH 43402
800–356–4219
www.electricquilt.com

PINKING SHEARS AND SCISSORS

Fiskars
2537 Daniels Street
Madison, WI 53718
866–348–5661
www.fiskars.com

BUBBLE JET SETTER

C. Jenkins Necktie & Chemical Company
39 S. Schlueter Ave.
Dellwood, MO 63135
314–521–7544 ext. 22
www.cjenkinscompany.com

BATTING AND FIBERFILL

Quilter's Dream
589 Central Drive
Virginia Beach, VA 23454
888–268–8664
www.quiltersdreambatting.com

St. Peter Woolen Mill
101 W. Broadway
St. Peter, MN 56082
800–208–9821

Warm Company
5529, 186th Place SW
Lynnwood, WA, 98037
425–248–2424
www.warmcompany.com

SPECIAL NOTIONS AND MILLINERY SUPPLIES

D. Blumchen & Co.
P.O. Box 1210-W
Ridgewood, NJ 07451
866–653–9627
www.blumchen.com

Manto Fev
402–505–3752
www.mantofev.com

Oregon Leather Company
110 NW 2nd Ave.
Portland, OR 97209
800–634–8033
www.oregonleatherco.com

SOFT TOY-MAKING SUPPLIES

BJ's Craft Supplies
203 Bickford Road
Tivoli, TX 77990
361–286–3366
www.bjcraftsupplies.com

Cloth Doll Supply
860–292–8591
www.clothdollsupply.com

Dollmaker's Journey
P.O. Box 523192
Springfield, VA 22152
www.dollmakersjourney.com

PHOTOGRAPHY

Two Peas in a Bucket
This scrapbooking website offers a series of online articles walking through the basics of digital photography and beyond
www.twopeasinabucket.com

Digicamhelp.com
www.digicamhelp.com

Digital Photography School
www.digital-photography-school.com/blog

BLOGGING

Artful Blogging
Print magazine devoted to profiling artistic blogs
www.stampington.com

Typepad
The service I use to build and maintain my blog
www.typepad.com

FOR FURTHER READING

New Complete Guide to Sewing
Readers Digest Editors
(Readers Digest: 2002)

Bend-the-Rules Sewing
Amy Karol
(Potter Craft: 2007)

Modern Quilt Workshop
Bill Kerr, Weeks Ringle
(Quarry Books: 2005)

Appliqué: The Basics and Beyond
Janet Pittman
(Landauer Corporation: 2006)

Decorative Embroidery
Mary Norden
(Readers Digest: 1997)

Templates

FAMILY TREE (PAGE 18):

Tree (use at 100%)

FAMILY TREE (PAGE 18):
(use all below at 100%)

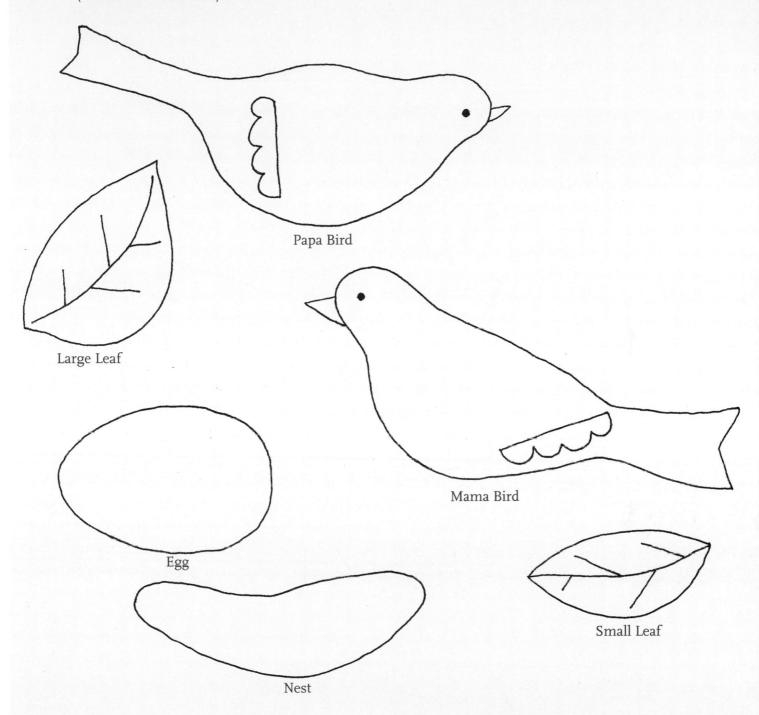

Papa Bird

Large Leaf

Egg

Mama Bird

Nest

Small Leaf

TOWNHOUSE GROWTH CHART (PAGE 35):
(use all below at 100%)

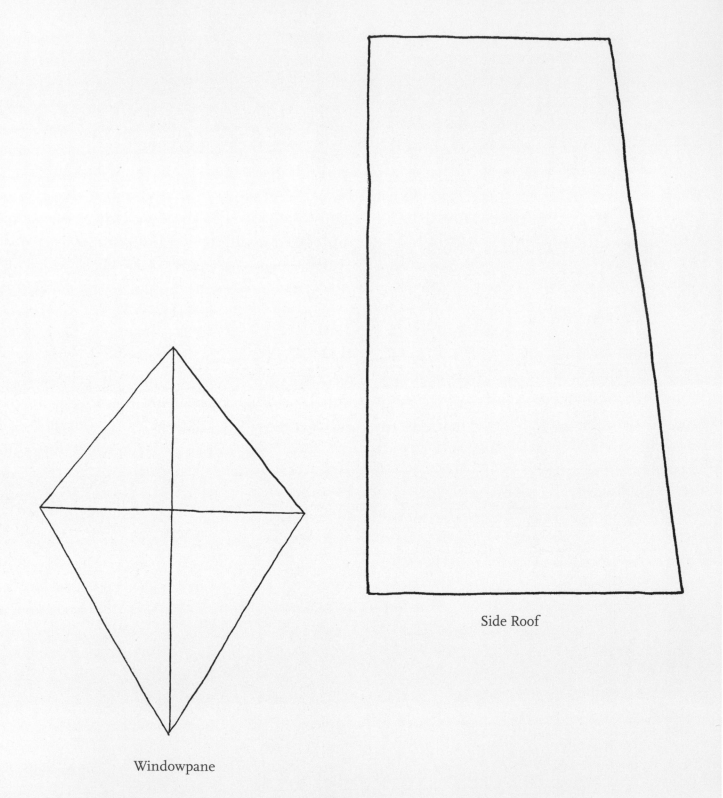

Side Roof

Windowpane

KID'S DRAWING SOFTIE (PAGE 43):
(use all below at 150%)

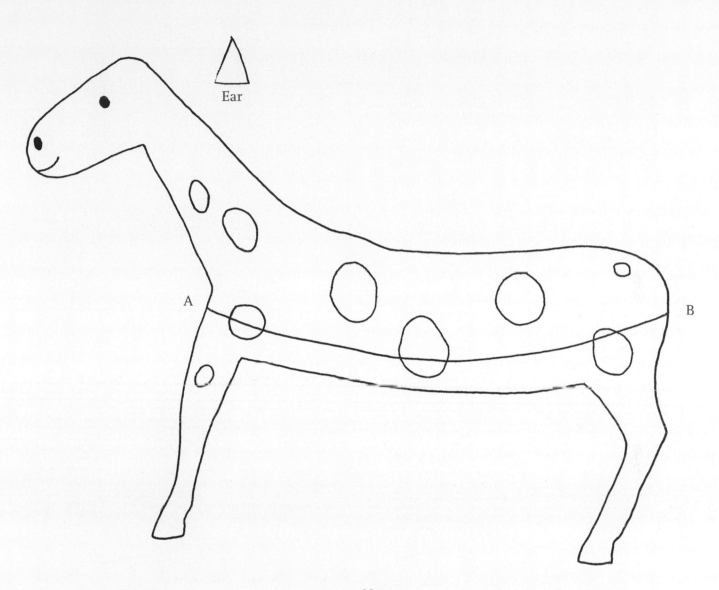

Ear

A

B

Horse

FRIEND CHANDELIER (PAGE 67):

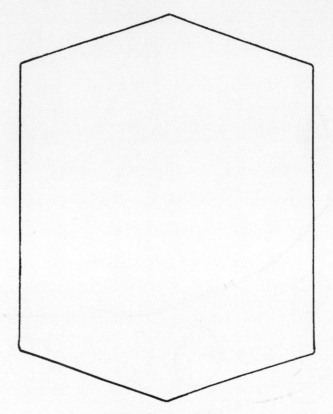

Crystal (use at 100%)

SNAIL ONESIE (PAGE 27):

Snail (use at 100%)

FAMILY RECIPE BOOK (PAGE 77):
(use all below at 100%)

Pot

Teacup

Spoon

Strainer

Cake

Strawberry

Knife

Baguette

BIRTHDAY BANNER (PAGE 98):

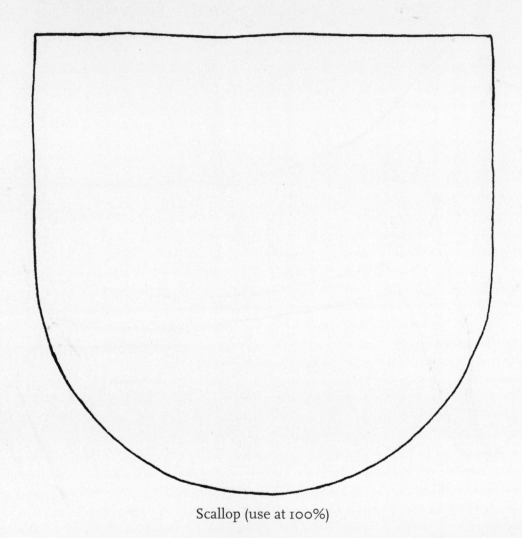

Scallop (use at 100%)

Heart (use at 100%)

NUTCRACKER DOLL (PAGE 104):

Head (use at 100%)

MONOGRAMMED STOCKING (PAGE 108):

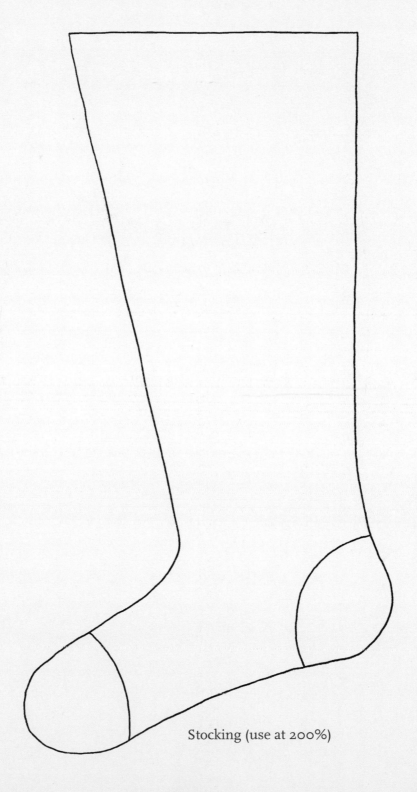

Stocking (use at 200%)

WEDDING REHEARSAL CORSAGE (PAGE 112):

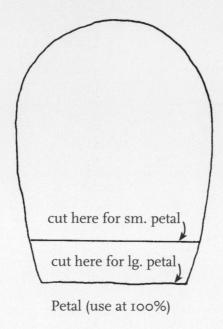

cut here for sm. petal

cut here for lg. petal

Petal (use at 100%)

HEART BUTTON RING PILLOW (PAGE 118):

Heart Button (use at 100%)

Wreath (use at 100%)

Alicia Paulson loves to make things. She spends her days in her home studio sewing, crocheting, embroidering, and designing a small, ever-changing collection of original crafts called Posie: Rosy Little Things. She loves horses, country fairs, the Oregon coast, apples, rock walls, Adirondack chairs, vintage china, fancy grocery stores, Miss Marple, cashmere-blend yarns, Thai food, vanilla beans, Puget Sound, Peter Pan collars, heart-shaped waffles, Scandinavian import stores, hot coffee, good conversation, laughing children, and old friends and writes about all of them daily at her blog, Posie Gets Cozy. She would like to create a sewing project that incorporates all of these inspirations at the same time.

Born and raised outside Chicago, she now lives in Portland, Oregon, with her husband, Nurse of the Year Andy Paulson, R.N.; two very bossy cats; and puppy Clover Meadow, the second-cutest Cardigan Welsh corgi in the world. Find them all at www.AliciaPaulson.com.

Acknowledgments

Thank you to my family: my parents, Al and Sue; my sisters, Julie and Susie; and my brother-in-law, Michael—the most creative people and the biggest dreamers I know. In our house, making things by hand was the happiest of habits, and books filled all my days.

Thank you to my extended family and friends, especially my mother-in-law, Suzan, but also Sarah and David, Shelly, Elizabeth and Stacy, Aimee, Martha, Jeanne-marie, and Jeff and JoEllen, whose enthusiasm for and interest in all my endeavors flatters and pleases me no end. Thank you also to Kristin Spurkland, Charlotte Lyons, Kristin Nicholas, and Leigh Radford, whose professionalism and generosity teach me so much.

Thank you to the incredible community of craft bloggers and blog readers who have welcomed me and my critters and my crafts and my flowery little corners every day for the past three years. Your attention has inspired me more than I can say. Thank you sincerely to Jane Brocket, Larissa Brown, Lisa Congdon, Melissa Frantz, Amy Karol, Hillary Lang, Leslie Lindell, Amy Powers, Amanda Soule, Blair Stocker, Toni and Hannah Weber, and Betz White. I'm grateful for and better because of your friendships.

Thank you to my agent Kate McKean, and to Courtney Conroy, Melissa Bonventre, and everyone at Potter Craft, especially Jennifer Graham, whose patience, skill, and generosity were invaluable. To Ellen Wheat, who got it all tidy and sparkling in the most important and invisible ways. And to Marysarah Quinn, whose design captures (so perfectly) everything I wanted to express.

Thank you to everyone who contributed time, effort, locations, props, beauty, humor, and pure effervescence to the photos that make these projects shine, especially to dearest Arden, and to Sarah K., Charlotte, Oliver, Caroline, Stephen, Miles, Cole, Sanju, Sarah G., April, the Palio Coffeehouse, Mike from Affordable Tire and Brake, and Nicole Walker, who makes everything look as lovely as she is.

And thank you, thanks beyond my abilities to express, to Andy Paulson, who in a million little ways per minute makes every single day one I want to remember. It's like having your life lit by shooting stars and birthday candles. Thank you, my love.

Index

Page numbers in *italics* indicate photos and templates.